BATTLE
IN THE AIR

Text
Michael C Tagg

Photography
Keystone Collection
Kristall Productions
TRH Pictures
UPI/Bettmann

Design
Clive Dorman

Commissioning Editor
Andrew Preston

Publishing Assistant
Edward Doling

Photo Research
Leora Kahn

Editorial
Jane Adams

Production
Ruth Arthur
David Proffit
Sally Connolly

Director of Production
Gerald Hughes

Director of Publishing
David Gibbon

MALLARD PRESS

An imprint of BDD Promotional Books Company, Inc,
666 Fifth Avenue, New York, N.Y. 10103.

Mallard Press and its accompanying design and logo
are trademarks of BDD Promotional Book Company, Inc.

CLB 2431
© 1990 Archive Publishing, a division of Colour Library Books Ltd,
Godalming, Surrey, England.
First published in the United States of America
in 1990 by The Mallard Press.
Printed and bound in Italy by New Interlitho.
All rights reserved.
ISBN 0 792 45375 1

WORLD WAR II

BATTLE IN THE AIR

MICHAEL C. TAGG

MALLARD PRESS

Second Lieutenant Kenneth A. Walsh, a U.S. Marine Corps fighter pilot who shot down sixteen enemy aircraft in the South Pacific.

CONTENTS

INTRODUCTION   6

THE BATTLES FOR NORWAY   12

COMBAT OVER DUNKIRK   21

BATTLE OF BRITAIN   31

THE DEFENCE OF MALTA   52

BATTLE OF TARANTO   64

INFAMY AT PEARL HARBOR   74

THE RISING SUN   86

THE DOOLITTLE RAID   95

AIR BATTLE FOR BURMA   104

ENTER THE MIGHTY 8TH   114

THE DAMBUSTERS   124

ATTACK ON SCHWEINFURT   133

PLOESTI - THE VITAL MISSION   144

THE MARIANAS TURKEY SHOOT   154

KAMIKAZE - THE DIVINE WIND   161

BIBLIOGRAPHY   176

INTRODUCTION

After World War I, as after other major wars, there were immediate demands for disarmament and for reductions in the armed forces. In most countries of the West this went beyond the reductions called for in the peace treaty. This did nothing to dampen the ardour of those promoting the development of aviation. The war had convinced everyone that flying was here to stay, and that the ability to fly, which man had acquired over the past fifteen years, could be put to a variety of practical purposes. So for the time being there was plenty of impetus for flying to be developed for peaceful uses. Throughout the 1920s the large aeroplane became larger, could fly further, and could carry greater loads. The small aeroplanes became faster, more reliable, and they also became capable of greater ranges.

During this period there was some development of military types, but most of the effort, actually or ostensibly, was devoted to civil applications.

As the world moved into the 1930s the advances in aviation technology began, more and more, to be applied to military aircraft. In 1931 both Britain and Japan produced fighter aircraft capable of speeds greater than 200 mph, with the Hawker Fury, and the Nakajima A2N Type 90 carrier fighter. Three years later Germany caught up, with the Heinkel He 51.

Meanwhile, the military aviators were developing new techniques which sometimes dictated the design of new aircraft types. The Americans pioneered the technique of dive bombing, enabling bombs to be delivered with much greater accuracy than was possible from high level with the bomb sighting equipment available at the time – in fact Britain entered World War II using a bomb sight which did not differ significantly from the one they had been using in 1918. Dive bombing

The Junkers Ju.52 (left) was conceived as a bomber and military transport in the late 1920s. However, after testing the machine during the Spanish Civil War, the Ju.52 was consigned solely to transport duties. In this pre-World War II photograph, the ventral gunner can be seen just aft of the fixed landing wheels in his exposed 'dustbin' gun position.

The Hawker Fury biplane (right) was the first RAF fighter to enter service with a top speed in excess of 200 mph. During the mid-1930s, Furies were famous mainly for their spectacular displays at the Hendon air pageant. Aspects of the design were later refined and employed in the development of the Hawker Hurricane.

The Hawker Hurricane (left), designed by Sydney Camm, was a vital addition to the prewar RAF's fighter command. Although the early version suffered teething problems, the Hurricane went on to destroy more enemy aircraft than the Spitfire in the first thirty months of the war.

America and Germany committed themselves to the development of dive-bombing techniques between the two world wars, designing aircraft specifically for the role. Germany's Junkers Ju.87 'Stuka' (below left) earned its spurs during the Spanish Civil War, and was to achieve greater renown - and notoriety - than any other dive bomber in World War II.

The biplane Henschel 123A (right) was Germany's first purpose-built dive bomber. It first flew in 1935, and entered service the following year. It saw action in Spain, and in the invasions of Poland and Western Europe, but it was phased out of its frontline role in favour of the Ju.87, which could carry almost ten times the bomb load.

eliminated the need for complicated equipment taking into account height and speed, the direction and speed of the wind, and even the free-fall characteristics of the bomb. The pilot simply aimed himself, and released the bomb at the appropriate moment. The characteristics of the ideal aircraft for this kind of attack were different from those for 'level' bombing, and soon aircraft were being designed specifically for this work.

The Americans were also first in the field with a multi-engined, retractable-undercarriage monoplane bomber, the Boeing B-9, which appeared in 1932. At about the same time Russia produced the Tupolev TB-3, which had four engines. Although slower than the B-9, it could carry twice the bomb load over twice the distance. There was a troop carrying version of the TB-3, which gave Russia the aircraft which carried the world's first airborne combat troops.

In the mid 1930s bomber aircraft were being built with performance equal, or even superior,

to that of the fighters of the day. The Russian Tupolev SB-2 was a twin-engined attack bomber capable of 260 mph, while the Italians had the Savoia-Marchetti S-79, a tri-motor machine with a speed of 270 mph. The S-79 was used mainly in a maritime role, carrying either bombs or torpedoes. It was held in such high esteem that its crews were regarded as the cream of the Italian Air Force.

Britain and Germany leapfrogged the fighter development of the other nations, and were the first air forces to specify the designs of heavily armed, all metal stressed-skin, high speed fighter aircraft. These specifications led to the Messerschmitt Bf 109 in Germany, and the Hawker Hurricane and the Supermarine Spitfire in Britain. The first versions of the British aircraft were armed with eight machine guns, while the Messerschmitt Bf 109 carried four machine guns and a 20mm cannon.

Conflicts which took place across the world during the 1930s showed an increasing use of air power, and demonstrated the use of some

techniques that were to become characteristic of World War II. In the war which broke out between China and Japan, late in 1931, the Japanese made extensive use of carrier-borne aircraft, and when Mussolini ordered the invasion of Ethiopia, during the Abyssinian War of 1935-36, mechanised troops were closely supported by aerial bombing. When sufficient incursions had been made, the aircraft were used extensively for the transport of troops and supplies.

But the conflict which became virtually a training ground for the aerial warfare of World War II was the Spanish Civil War, which began in July 1936.

When the uprising took place, in July 1936, the Spanish army on the mainland, by and large remained loyal to the Republican (Government) cause. Large numbers of Government troops serving with Arab volunteers in Morocco, however, threw in their hand with the Nationalists, but they were prevented from joining the conflict by the loyal Spanish navy. The insurgents appealed to Hitler and Mussolini for assistance, and Germany provided Junkers Ju 52 transports to ferry large numbers of troops to Spain. They were joined by Italian Savoia-Marchetti SM 80s, which also ferried troops, and were used to harass the Republican navy.

Initially the German and Italian personnel were present only as 'military advisers', but, dissatisfied with the performance of the Republican aircrews, who had defected to the Nationalist cause in large numbers from the Republican air force, they quickly obtained permission to take part in operations. Eventually the latest generation of German aircraft – the Messerschmitt Bf 109, Heinkel He 111 and Dornier Do 17 – were taking part, manned by German aircrews. Soon Germany was unashamedly

The Supermarine Spitfire was built to meet a specification, issued by the RAF in 1935, for an eight-gun fighter. The first prototype flew in 1936, but, because of production difficulties, it did not enter service, with 19 Squadron, until 1938. Through a series of different models it remained in frontline service until the end of World War II, and was arguably the outstanding fighter of the war.

The Dornier Do.17 was, at the time of its appearance, one of the fastest reconnaissance aircraft in the world. Following frontline experience in the Spanish Civil War, it was almost completely redesigned, and went on to become a mainstay of the Luftwaffe bombing arm, seeing service throughout World War II.

using the war as a training opportunity, rotating their aircrews so that, eventually, most of the crews of their operational types had had actual war experience.

An outstanding lesson learned by Germany during the Spanish Civil War was the effectiveness of the dive-bomber in support of the army, especially when, towards the end of 1937, the Junkers Ju 87 'Stuka' began to appear.

For a considerable period the 'Kondor Legion', as the German air force units operating in Spain were known, enjoyed air supremacy. They came to believe that they would always be able to operate their fast medium bomber formations with the support of only light fighter escort. They were able to retain this belief for almost the whole of the first year of World War II, but it began to be shaken in the summer of 1940.

The development of radio techniques during the 1930s were to have a significant effect upon air operations during World War II. Air-to-air and ground-to-air communication was developed to a practical standard, making a great difference in air fighting, and in the ability of ground forces to summon and direct air support.

Perhaps the most important of all was the development of radio-location, RADAR, particularly in Britain, where, as a result of experiments begun in 1934, a usable chain of detection stations had been set up by 1938. As part of the development of civil aviation, the use of radio beacons on the ground, for both navigation and airfield approach purposes, was well established. The beacons on the ground were interrogated by equipment in the aircraft, and interpreted by the aircrew, a situation which was not to change significantly until well after World War II.

THE BATTLES FOR NORWAY

The British Gloster Gladiator was an 'in between' fighter. With the biplane appearance of a World War I aircraft, it also had some of the features of one. As well as being the RAF's last biplane fighter, it was also the last to have a fixed undercarriage, and, with two of its four machine guns mounted inside the engine cowling, it was the last to have armament synchronised to fire through the arc of the propeller. On the other hand, it was one of the first to be of all-metal construction, the first to have fixed machine guns mounted in the wings, outside the propeller arc, and the first to offer its pilot the comfort of an enclosed cockpit.

In the early summer of 1940 Gladiators were to earn an undying reputation in the defence of the Mediterranean island fortress of Malta. However, earlier in the year, before the snows had thawed in Norway, on the fringes of the Arctic Circle, Gladiators had been involved in equally heroic and much more poignant action.

On April 7 the Germans had invaded Denmark and Norway. They obtained control of Denmark, almost bloodlessly, very quickly. Norway managed to hold out against the first onslaught, so that there was time for Britain to make plans to help out. The British had a significant vested interest in preventing Norway from falling into German hands. A foothold in Norway would give Germany an extremely useful base from which to carry out both air and sea operations against the northeast corner of the United Kingdom. The German forces were concentrated in the south of Norway, trying to push north. If their small force

Both sides in the Norwegian campaign used frozen lakes as ready-made forward airfields. These Luftwaffe ground crew (left) seem unconcerned about the cold as they load a bomb beneath a Junkers Ju.87.

The Heinkel He.111, with its characteristic glazed nose, was in the forefront of all of Germany's invasions. The front gunner (right) reclines behind his optically flat glass panel, beneath his pilot's feet.

holding a beachhead at Trondheim could be thrown back into the sea, the British could regroup with the Norwegians to begin to push back southwards. A pincer movement was planned, with landings to the north and south of Trondheim, with the two groups moving together to cut off the invading garrison. What the troops really needed, to help them resist any counterattack, was air cover.

The aircraft carrier HMS *Glorious* had been brought back from the Mediterranean to help out nearer to home, and she was despatched to Norway carrying No. 263 Squadron of the Royal Air Force, with their Gladiator fighters. When they left England no airfield in Norway had been selected. A Gladiator squadron was sent in case the base should turn out to be too small for the more modern aircraft. In fact, this was just as well. The RAF Advance Party arrived

on April 22, and selected as their base the frozen Lake Lesjaskog, some miles inland from the small port of Aandalsnes, to the south of Trondheim. A working party of 200 local civilians was recruited, and they set about the task of removing the snow from the surface of the Lake, to create a runway. Forty-eight hours later a signal was sent to *Glorious* to say that they were ready for the Gladiators. The carrier was still 180 miles off shore, it was snowing, and before leaving England they had been able to obtain only four maps of the area – less than one to each four aircraft. None of them had ever taken off from an aircraft carrier, they carried no navigational equipment other than the basic blind-flying panel, and they had to find a small lake, tucked in among the mountains, which no one had seen before. Their leader saw little likelihood of them making

a successful landfall. The Captain of *Glorious* offered to send a Skua, a two-seat strike aircraft, to lead them in. With this assistance they got off the carrier without mishap, and all landed safely at Lesjaskog. As they flew over Aandalsnes a British soldier unloading supplies on the dockside remarked, 'Here come our fighters. Now the bombers are in trouble.' The C.O. of 263 Squadron did not share his confidence. He had already spotted that the Luftwaffe roamed at will over the area, and it was clear that they had noticed the preparation of the runway. The aircraft were dispersed around the airfield for safety, and the pilots snatched a brief sleep until the early daylight of the northern latitudes.

Their disillusionment came with the dawn. They were scheduled to carry out a patrol at 3 a.m. In fact, it was two hours later before the first pair made it into the air. The severe overnight cold had frozen the carburettors and controls, and the wheels were iced to the surface of the lake. As the morning progressed their plight was spotted by the enemy, and relays of Junkers Ju.88s, and Heinkel He.111s flew over, again and again. Subjected to continuous bombing and gunfire, the ground crews struggled to free more aircraft, and at the same time to refuel and rearm those that had already got into the air. It was a losing battle. By midday ten of the eighteen Gladiators had been destroyed on the ground. The remaining aircraft were flown continuously. They engaged in frequent combats, and shot down a number of the enemy, but by evening only five aircraft remained, and the surface of the lake was merely a waste of splintered ice.

The remnants of the shattered squadron withdrew to an emergency landing ground on a plateau above Aandalsnes. The five Gladiators flew one more sortie together the next morning. Three returned. They tried, independently, to interfere with the German aircraft attacking the port, but, by midday only one aircraft remained, and that only partially serviceable. There was no longer any point in them staying in Norway. The pilots boarded a cargo ship leaving Aandalsnes, and, surviving a series of air attacks, they arrived back in

The Royal Navy's carrier-based fighter-bomber, the Blackburn Skua. Because 263 Squadron's Gladiators carried nothing more than a magnetic compass to facilitate long-range navigation, Skuas from HMS *Glorious* acted as shepherds when the Gladiators left the carrier to fly to their bases in Norway.

The Luftwaffe allocated 600 combat aircraft for the invasion of Norway. A significant number of them were Heinkel He.111s. This dramatic formation is typical of those seen in Norwegian skies during 1940.

Scotland – a mere ten days after they had left.

Central Norway was abandoned. The Norwegian and British troops, now reinforced by French units, set about the task of preventing the Germans advancing any further north.

On May 21, 263 Squadron returned, carried this time by HMS *Furious*, with a fresh supply of Gladiators. Directed even further north than during their previous foray, the weather was no better than before. This time a Navy Swordfish acted as shepherd, but the visibility was so bad that he crashed into a mountainside as they crossed the coast, and was followed by the first two Gladiators. The rest managed to avoid the hazard and turned back to try to find the carrier, and face the further peril of their first carrier landing.

The next day conditions improved. The Gladiators came ashore and established themselves at Bardufoss. On that day they flew almost fifty sorties before the daylight faded.

The strategy now was that the Allies should attempt to reoccupy the port of Narvik, solely in order to destroy the harbour installation. The whole force would then withdraw, ready to take part in the even more important task of defending against the imminent German attack in the west. The assault on Narvik would take place as soon as 263 Squadron had been reinforced by a squadron of Hurricanes. On May 26 they arrived, and on the 27th the two squadrons began to fly patrols over Narvik. In the afternoon the attack began. Throughout the next day the Gladiators and Hurricanes fought off the attentions of Junkers Ju.87s, diving to support the defenders, and by evening the town had fallen.

Between May 29 and June 1 the work of the

One squadron of RAF Hurricanes (left), together with the squadron of Gladiators and some Royal Navy fighters from the aircraft carriers HMS *Ark Royal* and HMS *Glorious*, fought a losing battle over Norway to deny air superiority to the Luftwaffe.

The Luftwaffe's twin-engined long-range fighter, the Messerschmitt Bf.110 (right), preceded the troop-carrying Junkers Ju.52s to achieve command of the air over Oslo and Stavanger.

A Royal Navy Fairey Swordfish (below right), its wings folded, is struck down to the hangar deck of its carrier. A Swordfish from HMS *Glorious* guided the Gladiators of 263 Squadron to the carrier when they were evacuated from Norway.

British proceeded in the port, while the two squadrons fended off the sporadic German attacks. Then, on June 2, the Luftwaffe appeared in force. Wave after wave of massed bombers, escorted by Messerschmitt Bf.110s, attempted to destroy the British shipping. But every attack was so harassed by the fighters that the German crews' aim was careless, or they jettisoned their bombs wide of the target. By the end of the day the two squadrons had flown almost eighty sorties, fought twenty-four engagements, and had destroyed at least nine enemy aircraft.

That evening the Norwegians were told of the British intention to withdraw, and the next morning the evacuation began. The embarkation would have presented tempting targets for the Germans, but the weather was kind to the defenders, and few attacks developed. Those raids which did appear were comfortably contained by the fighters, helped now by Naval aircraft from Glorious and Furious, which had returned to help with the evacuation.

The Royal Air Force was operating under specific instructions to fly patrols over the vital areas until the evacuation was virtually complete. The Gladiators were then to re-embark on Glorious, and the Hurricanes, which it was thought would not be able to accomplish the carrier landing, were to be destroyed. Aware of the desperate need for Hurricanes back in Britain, the Hurricane squadron commander begged that his pilots be allowed to put themselves at risk in an attempt to save the aircraft. His request was granted, and every pilot in the squadron responded to the invitation to volunteer to make the attempt. In the evening of June 7 the Gladiators successfully landed on, and were safely stowed below decks by the time the Hurricanes took off from Bardufoss. An hour later they had caught up with the carrier, its two attendant destroyers standing by to attempt to snatch from the arctic waters any pilot who was not successful. Their services were not required; every Hurricane landed safely.

If this had been the end of the story, it would have been a happy ending. But this was not to be.

The German Navy had a raiding party at sea. The battle-cruisers Scharnhorst and Gneisenau, with the cruiser Hipper, had been instructed to patrol the seas around Narvik, to prey upon the British shipping withdrawing from Norway. At 4 p.m. on the day after they had sailed from Narvik, Glorious and her destroyer escort fell foul of the raiders. The carrier's 4-inch guns were useless at the range of 27,000 yards at which the enemy opened fire. She attempted to launch her torpedo-carrying Swordfish to retaliate, but was frustrated by early hits from the German vessels. Within one hour, all three of the British ships were sunk. The Royal Navy lost 1,474 officers and men.

For once the pilots of 263 Squadron, and their friends from the Hurricane squadron, had been faced by an enemy against whom they could not respond. The leader of the Hurricane squadron, with one of his pilots, was among the thirty-nine survivors who were picked up the next day. Of the Gladiator pilots of 263 Squadron there was no trace.

The German battle-cruiser *Scharnhorst*, with its partner *Gneisenau*, was a constant influence on the campaign in Norway, where all supplies and reinforcements had to be brought in by sea. The two cruisers brought about a disaster when they intercepted HMS *Glorious* as she was evacuating the Hurricanes and Gladiators of 46 and 263 Squadrons.

COMBAT OVER DUNKIRK

The Messerschmitt Bf.109 was the aircraft which ensured that the Luftwaffe retained air superiority both during the *Blitzkrieg* days, and over the beaches of Dunkirk. Operating close to its forward airfields, it was able to remain in the operational area for considerable periods, and outclassed all its opposition until the RAF's Spitfires began to take part in the fray.

As the Allied armies were forced back towards towards the coasts of Belgium and northern France, the French Air Force ceased to be effective, and the air component of the British Expeditionary Force, to avoid being overrun on its airfields in France, was withdrawn to England.

Operating from the comparative safety of its established bases on home soil, its task was threefold. The bombers and reconnaissance aircraft, with fighter escort during daylight, carried out operations to delay the German advance which was squeezing the troops within an ever shrinking perimeter. The fighters flew patrols to give air cover to the beleaguered soldiers and, because the Luftwaffe now had access to airfields from which Britain was not

much more then a stones throw away, were standing by to provide air defence for the homeland.

Close escort of the bomber formations had not previously been considered necessary. The theory was that the bombers could take care of themselves except over the target, where they would need fighter support to have the sky swept clear of hostile aircraft, because here the bomber crews would be too busy with their primary function to be concerned with self-defence. This was fine in theory, but in practice the fighters over the target area were often outnumbered by as much as five or six to one. When the bombers arrived the fighters were too busy fighting for their own lives to afford

them any protection. All that they really achieved was that their arrival warned the enemy that a bombing raid was on the way! On May 17 twelve Blenheims of 82 Squadron were briefed to attack advancing German columns. Hurricanes were already in position over the target, but the Blenheims were jumped by fifteen Bf.109s while still en route. Without fighter escort all but one were shot down.

Having decided that the 'coup de grace' to the retreating allies, penned into their pocket around Dunkirk, should be delivered by the Luftwaffe, Hitler called a halt to the advance of the rampant panzers. However, the Luftwaffe found that, for once, it was confronted by opposition which had the power to resist. The turret fighter, the Boulton Paul Defiant, came into the fray, and for the moment the Luftwaffe had no tactics to take care of it. Much more significant, one of the classic confrontations of World War II began. For the first time the Messerschmitt Bf.109 came face to face with the Supermarine Spitfire. During the Battle of France it had been held in reserve by the Royal Air Force. A New Zealand pilot flying a Spitfire with 54 Squadron reported, 'As a result of my

The Bolton Paul Defiant, with its four .303 machine guns in a power-operated turret, enjoyed a brief heyday when it first appeared over Dunkirk. Caught by surprise, the Luftwaffe quickly developed techniques to deal with this opponent, which was soon withdrawn from the day-fighter role.

As Germany's *Blitzkrieg* swept across Europe, the light bombers of the French, Belgian and British air forces faced overwhelming odds in an effort to stem the tide. Two squadrons of RAF Bristol Blenheims were wiped out in two days, as Germany advanced unchecked towards Dunkirk.

prolonged fight with the 109, I was able to assess the relative performance of the two aircraft. In early engagements with Hurricanes the speed and climb of the 109s had become legendary, and were claimed by many to be far superior to the Spitfire. I was able to refute this. I was confident that, except in a dive, the Spitfire was superior in most areas, and, like the Hurricane, vastly more manoeuvrable.'

From their bases in southern England, the British fighters operated standing patrols over the French coast from Calais to Boulogne, waiting for the German bombers to arrive. The

Royal Air Force had a book of tactics which told them what to do next – and they had been practicing it for years. 'Formation attack Number Five, go!', cried the Squadron Commander when the bombers appeared, and the Spitfires moved smoothly into the formation which had thrilled crowds of spectators watching their summer manoeuvres in previous years. Unfortunately, the book had not taken into account the swarm of Bf.109s which would dive out of the sun, and within seconds the pretty formations had scattered into a chaotic free-for-all. And so another chapter of the

peacetime rule book went out of the window.

One Spitfire pilot noted, 'What a day; up at 3.30 a.m., four patrols involving seven-and-a-half hours flying, two engagements, and I finished up with three enemy aircraft to my credit.' This set the pattern for the days that followed. The victories were not gained without loss. On May 15, 54 Squadron had joined the battle with sixteen aircraft and twenty-four pilots. By May 26 they were reduced to five aircraft and ten pilots. Making a superhuman effort during the night, the ground crews produced eight serviceable aircraft for the first patrol next morning, when two more aircraft and pilots were lost. The squadron was withdrawn to recoup, and took no further part in the battle.

The true state of things on the ground was not being made public. The fighter pilots knew only what they read in the newspapers, that 'a planned withdrawal' was being made from some areas. From the air they saw little of it. For the most part they were operating above the cloud, and the pall of black smoke from the burning oil installations of Dunkirk, which had hung over the area for days. One pilot who survived a crash landing on the beach when he was shot down was horrified to learn the true state of things. He was also taken aback by the hostility he faced from the troops, especially when, hurrying to get back to England to collect another Spitfire, he jumped the queue waiting to board the next destroyer. For a week he had

The RAF's Hawker Hurricanes (below) bore the brunt of the fighting as the Allies fell back before the *Blitzkrieg*. The RAF were loath to risk the limited number of Spitfires operating from airfields in France. Throughout the evacuation from Dunkirk, Spitfire squadrons (right) crossed the Channel from southern England to defend the beachhead.

As the harbour at Dunkirk became blocked and its quays damaged, the troops sheltered among the sand dunes or lined up (left) on the beaches, waiting their turn to be picked up by the small boats that would carry them to the transports waiting offshore.

The larger vessels moved as close as they could to the beach (right), but the troops could not wade out far enough to embark. At low tide trucks, due to be abandoned, were driven down the beach to form a makeshift pier. As the water rose again the embarkation proceeded.

been risking his life four times a day to protect the beachhead.

Not only had most of the air combat taken place out of sight of the men on the beaches and on the ships rescuing them, but the Royal Air Force were heavily outnumbered, and though they destroyed two of the enemy for each loss of their own, there were plenty of attackers left to wreak havoc on Dunkirk. Little surprise, then, that as the exhausted soldiers clambered onto the quayside at Dover, the first question asked by most of them was, 'Where was the R.A.F.?' Even Vice-Admiral Ramsey, Flag Officer Dover, responsible for the overall

execution of the evacuation, wrote, 'Full air protection was expected, but for hours on end ships were subjected to a murderous hail of bombs and machine-gun bullets. The C.Os of many ships reported their disappointment at the seemingly puny efforts to provide protection.'

By the last few days of May it had become useless to pretend that a disaster had not happened in France. The train loads of bedraggled soldiers being moved away from Dover, most of them without equipment, told their own story. Once the need for security was relaxed, an armada of privately-owned

pleasure craft came forward to help with the evacuation. Hundreds of small craft, some only able to carry ten or twelve men, made their way across the Channel to Dunkirk. They were invaluable in ferrying troops from the beaches to the larger craft which could not get close inshore.

By midday on June 4 everything which could be done had been done. Almost 400,000 men had been rescued. It would be just over four years before Allied troops returned to France, except for Commando raids and clandestine operations.

Churchill's own history of World War II records that a major factor in the success of the evacuation was the work of the Royal Air Force. Day after day they fought the enemy at long odds. Wherever German aircraft were encountered, sometimes in forties and fifties, they were instantly attacked, often by a single squadron or less, and shot down in numbers. He records that the troops on the beaches saw little of this conflict, and knew little of the losses inflicted on the Germans. All they were aware of was the bombing on the beaches. Men landing at Dover or at the Thames ports often insulted men in Royal Air Force uniform. 'They should have clasped them by the hand,' said Churchill, 'but how could they know?'

A Hurricane pilot, wearing his flying helmet, life jacket and parachute, and with his 'Sutton' cockpit harness ready to fasten him into his seat, examines the progress of the preparation of his aircraft for another sortie.

While the RAF fought to protect the perimeter of the beachhead, the only aircraft seen by the soldiers waiting to embark were those of the enemy that broke through. As the Stukas dived down upon them, they took the opportunity to use up what little ammunition they had left (right).

Once on board ship, the soldiers were not necessarily safe. Seventy-two ships, including nine destroyers, were sunk by the German bombers. Below right: soldiers wear crude cork buoyancy aids as they watch the smoke of the Dunkirk oil depot recede.

British Prime Minister, Mr. Winston Churchill. 'I expect the Battle of Britain is about to begin,' he said after the fall of France, coining the name by which the world's first great battle to be fought entirely in the air was to become known.

BATTLE OF BRITAIN

The Battle of Britain was to be the prelude to 'Operation Sealion', the invasion of Britain. The Local Defence Volunteers, soon to be renamed The Home Guard, began training to support the full-time army. Anti-aircraft fire was part of their training - but it was carried out without using any ammunition.

The rescue of over 300,000 men from the beaches of Dunkirk was a tremendous achievement. Without it World War Two might have been over there and then. On 1 June 1940 *The New York Times* declared, 'So long as the English tongue survives, the word Dunkirk will be spoken with reverence. In that harbour – such a hell as never blazed on earth before – at the end of a lost battle, the rags and blemishes that had hidden the soul of democracy fell away. There, beaten but unconquered, she (England) faced the enemy, this shining thing in the souls of free men which Hitler cannot command. It is the great tradition of democracy. It is the future. It is victory.'

But British Prime Minister Winston Churchill,

with one of his most outstanding speeches, drove home to his people that this had not been a victory, only a spark of triumph at the end of a crushing defeat. ' ... the Battle of France is over. I expect that the Battle of Britain is about to begin.', he warned, coining the term which was to become a milestone in the history of air warfare.

The battle of France had been a land battle, although air supremacy had played a vital part in its outcome. Churchill's assurance that 'we shall fight on the beaches, we shall fight on the landing grounds, in the fields, in the streets, and in the hills', suggests he expected that the Battle of Britain would be mainly a land battle also. How could he know that it would be an air

battle? At that time there had never been a battle fought entirely in the air.

Germany was riding on the crest of a wave. Everything had gone according to plan – or even better. In a little over two months the whole of mainland Western Europe had been overrun. All that stood between them and the total domination of the area was Great Britain. The best part of three months remained before the autumn gales would make the narrow sea crossing difficult, and cause the invasion of Britain to be delayed until 1941.

Germany would adopt the usual plan. The total annihilation of the opposing air force, followed by a rapid advance on the ground, with close air support to break up local pockets of resistance. The English Channel would be treated as just another river, and so far the Wehrmacht had taken rivers in their stride. Admittedly it was a bit wider than the others.

Bridges were out of the question, and everyone would have to go by boat or by air. So there was also going to be the possibility of a hostile navy taking a hand in proceedings. The German Combined Staffs admitted that they did not have total command of the sea, but they decreed that this would not matter once they had established supremacy in the air. So, at least in the opening stages, this was going to be an air battle.

After Dunkirk a number of German aircraft were retained on airfields in northern France to harry the sea ports in the south of England, and the shipping in the English Channel, disrupting the delivery of much needed supplies to Britain. However, the majority of Luftwaffe units were withdrawn to Germany to rest and re-equip.

Meanwhile, Britain prepared to repel an invasion. The army had brought back large numbers of men from France, but the bulk of

The Luftwaffe's long-range fighter, the Messerschmitt Bf.110, was the only fighter with the ability to escort the bombers throughout their sorties over England. They were unable to match either the Spitfire or the Hurricane in combat, and had to rely upon the tactic of forming a defensive circle to fight a rearguard action whilst the bombers made their escape.

The Heinkel He.111, the mainstay of the Luftwaffe's bombing effort during the Battle of Britain, was another German combat aircraft that had cut its teeth during the Spanish Civil War.

their equipment had been left behind. A great deal of re-equipping and retraining had to be done before they would be ready to face an invader. To help out, a 'citizens army' was formed. The 'Local Defence Volunteers', soon renamed the 'Home Guard', consisted of those who were too young, too old, or those considered unfit to serve in the regular forces. Members of the Home Guard were equipped with few modern or automatic weapons, often with no ammunition, and even with some obsolete arms from World War One or earlier, and often nothing more than farm implements or wooden replica rifles with which to carry out their drills. For many years they were the butt of music hall humour.

The air defence of Great Britain was to be the responsibility of the Royal Air Force's Fighter Command, led by Air Chief Marshal Sir Hugh Dowding. Dowding was an elderly ex-soldier who had seen operational flying in France during World War One, and who had already been warned that his retirement date was approaching. Perhaps this knowledge had helped his determination when, during the days before Dunkirk, he had confronted Churchill and the War Cabinet, resolutely refusing to allow any more of his single-engine fighter squadrons, the vital Spitfires and Hurricanes, to be sent to almost certain doom in France. What had he to lose except, perhaps, the war? 'I would remind you', he said, 'that the last estimate as to the forces necessary to defend this country was 52 Squadrons, and my strength has now been reduced to the equivalent of 36 Squadrons.'

Air Chief Marshal Sir Hugh Dowding, commander in chief of RAF Fighter Command. Dowding, a veteran of World War I, was due to leave the RAF in 1940. His retirement date was progressively deferred until the Battle of Britain had been won. He was then sent to the United States on a liaison mission.

Fighter Command was not alone in being commanded by a World War I veteran. Reichmarshal Herman Goering (right) had already had a distinguished career as a fighter pilot on the Western Front.

The pilots of 601 'County of London' Squadron (below right) play cricket whilst 'at readiness', waiting for the order to 'scramble'. The fitters sit in the Hurricanes, ready to start the engines as soon as the bell rings.

His command was divided geographically into Groups. Number 11 Group, under Air Vice-Marshal Keith Park, guarded London and the south east counties. They would bear the brunt of the attacks. The immediate support would be provided by Air Vice-Marshal Trafford Leigh-Mallory's Number 12 Group, based in the midland counties, to their north.

The respite before the onslaught, whilst Hitler waited to see if Britain would take fright and sue for peace, provided valuable breathing space for the RAF to lick its wounds from France, and to prepare for what was to come. The aircraft factories worked furiously to supply aircraft. After Dunkirk Dowding's operational squadrons could muster no more than 330 Hurricanes and Spitfires. Only 36 more were available in storage for issue as replacements. Eight weeks later, when the Battle began, the squadrons had over 600 aircraft, and almost 300 more were in reserve.

Pilots were a different matter. France had seen the loss of 300 fighter pilots, and these had been the cream. The front line was made up to strength by bringing young men early from the training schools. They were going to polish their craft the hard way. The Royal Navy loaned 58 pilots from the Fleet Air Arm, one squadron was manned by the Royal Canadian Air Force, and four squadrons by men who had escaped to Britain from the decimated air forces of Poland and Czechoslovakia. The Air Staff now estimated that Dowding would need 120 squadrons for his task. He still had no more than 60, and there was no chance of making up the difference. To make matters worse there was a shortage of anti-aircraft guns. Before the war the Chiefs of Staff had specified a requirement of 4,000 guns. A more recent review had doubled this. There were only 2,000, and the factories could turn out no more than 40 each month.

The one redeeming feature was radar, or 'RDF', – radio direction finding – as it was called at that time. Germany was aware of its existence, and had been keeping an eye upon

A team of four armourers could rearm a Spitfire in under ten minutes. This entailed replacing the empty ammunition boxes with full ones, feeding the belts of ammunition through, cleaning out the barrels, and cocking the guns. This particular Spitfire belonged to 610 'County of Chester' Squadron.

The Junkers Ju.87 (right) had been a star performer in Spain, Poland and Western Europe. However, it was found to be vulnerable over Britain, where the Luftwaffe did not have air superiority, and its use there was limited.

Two Hurricanes (overleaf) of 501 'County of Gloucester' Squadron take off to join in the fighting of Sunday, September 15, 1940. This was the day on which the battle reached its climax; the day which, ever since, has been commemorated as 'Battle of Britain Day'.

its progress since before the beginning of the war. Fortunately for Britain they did not fully appreciate its potential, nor fully realise how it was to be employed. By the standards of fifty years later it was ludicrously crude. In 1940 it was a principle that had been discovered only a few years earlier. It bore no resemblance to the 'plan position indicator' so familiar today, with a screen showing a map of the area covered, and a speck of light indicating each aircraft within range. This was no more than a trace on an oscilloscope. From a peak in the trace the operator had to estimate the direction and range of the target, and decide whether it represented a single aircraft or a formation. It was already possible to identify which traces were created by friendly aircraft, but the equipment looked in one direction only – out to sea. Once a raider, or a defender, had crossed the coast and was flying over the land, its progress could be tracked only by visual observation, or, at night, by its sound.

The stage was set.

By mid-July the Luftwaffe had returned from Germany. Lined up on the airfields in France and Belgium were 2,600 aircraft. Of these, 1,200 were long range bombers, with 1,000 escort fighters. Their task, within the general orders for the invasion of Britain, issued at that time, was twofold. They were to eliminate the RAF in the air, and disrupt its ground organisation, and they were to strangle the flow of supplies to Britain by stepping up the attacks on its ports and shipping. This latter effort was to begin at once. The onslaught upon the RAF would begin early in August, on a date to be decided, and was to be code named 'Eagle Day'. In its previous campaigns the Luftwaffe had taken between 12 and 48 hours to dispose of any air force which had confronted it. In acknowledgement of the fact that the RAF was the most powerful opponent yet, three to four weeks were allowed for its destruction, so the invasion, code named 'Sea Lion', would begin during the first two weeks of September.

The size and frequency of raids against ports and shipping built up, with occasional attacks against the airfields and the radar stations in the coastal area, and the Germans began to probe Britain's air defences. Large formations of fighters carried out sweeps over southern England, and small formations of bombers, with heavy fighter escorts, raided targets just inland from the coast. The object was to bring the RAF into combat, and to begin the attrition which would destroy Fighter Command.

There was more than one way of bringing down the enemy. There were a number of instances of pilots who were out of ammunition intentionally colliding with their adversary. A leading aircraftman of the ground crew examines the wing tip of a Hurricane which has been clipped in a collision with an enemy aircraft.

The original wartime caption to this July 1940 photograph identifies the pilot as Sergeant Corfe, seen here at the controls of his Spitfire, ready to return to the battle above.

A Spitfire breaks away to pass beneath a 'Flying Pencil'. It was usually the Hurricanes which were directed to attack the bombers, whilst the faster and more agile Spitfires provided top cover to fend off the Messerschmitt Bf.109s.

With the attacks taking place only over the coast, the RAF received insufficient early warning to gain a height advantage, and were always entering combat from below their opponents. And they quickly discovered that the tight formations of their 1930s air show manoeuvres were not ideal when the opposition meant business. They quickly learned to fly much looser formations, what became the classic 'finger four', giving better mutual protection – a lesson which had been learned by the Germans in the Kondor Legion in Spain.

The Luftwaffe found that they were not gaining the upper hand they had anticipated, and they began to probe deeper into British territory, in order to extend the time during which they could engage the defending fighters. But this only gave the fighters more time to gain height, and the results did not significantly improve.

The long-range escort fighter, the twin-engine Messerschmitt Bf.110, proved to be short of speed and manoeuvrability, and they were unhappy when confronted by Hurricanes and Spitfires. The Luftwaffe single-engine fighters found that they had to escort them, as well as the bombers. Not only that, but the RAF retaliated with unexpected aggression and pursued the bombers far out to sea, so that the Germans had to keep fighters in reserve to escort them home. The German fighter pilots were finding things more difficult than they had in the past.

But it was not just the Luftwaffe that was finding life hard. Fighter Command's pilots were under severe strain. Three or four sorties a day was the usual demand, six or seven was not

uncommon, and on most occasions they found themselves at a grave disadvantage. Not only were they attacking an enemy who usually had the advantage of height, but a mere handful of Hurricanes or Spitfires frequently found themselves engaged in mortal combat with formations of a hundred or more German aircraft. Leigh-Mallory, of 12 Group, supported the tactic of getting his aircraft into the air and forming them into 'big wings' before entering combat, but this took time. Park, with his 11 Group in the front line, could not afford the luxury of getting his squadrons airborne and into wings in anticipation of an attack, in case

they were in the wrong place, or beginning to run short of fuel when the attack developed. By the time he had warning of a raid, there was just no time.

In the period from 10 July until 10 August around 100 of Fighter Commands aircraft were shot down, but they had accounted for well over twice that number of Germans. This advantage was enhanced because the RAF was fighting over its home territory. If a pilot was shot down, and survived uninjured, he was soon back in the fray. A well-respected summary of the battle, published thirty years later, records a Hurricane pilot, shot down by a Bf.109 and

The people of southern England were able to watch the Battle of Britain being fought above their heads. When the aircraft were too high to be seen by the naked eye, their movements could be discerned in the tracery of vapour trails left in the sky.

Another Luftwaffe victim of the battle. This Messerschmitt Bf.109 has crash-landed, but is relatively undamaged, embedded in the shingle, somewhere on the coast of England.

slightly wounded, himself shooting down a Bf.109 just three-and-a-half-hours later.

Meanwhile, the Luftwaffe was beginning to build up night bombing, in addition to the daylight raids. Their main night targets were the British aircraft industry, to disrupt the supply of replacements to Fighter Command, and the airfields of RAF Bomber Command. As well as delivering probing attacks into Germany itself, and beginning to seek out and attack the build-up of troop-carrying barges in the Channel ports, Bomber Command's aircraft were attacking the German front line airfields, and interfering with their conduct of the battle. The night activity did not particularly affect the RAF's day fighters, but it did put extra strain on the raid reporting and fighter control organisation, and on the thinly spread anti-aircraft guns.

And the concentrated attack on the RAF had yet to begin.

'Eagle Day' had been provisionally set for 10 August, but, because of unfavourable weather forecasts, this had been put back to 13 August. However, the RAF must have been aware of a change of tactics on the 12th. Early in the morning the Germans launched fierce attacks against the radar stations in the southeast corner of England, so that by 9 o'clock there was a gap in the early-warning system stretching from Dover to beyond the Isle of Wight. Undetected now, a series of further raids were assembled over France, including one of over 200 aircraft, briefed to attack targets throughout the southeast area, including three of the RAF's airfields in the coastal area.

By an enormous effort, all but one of the radar stations were operating again by the evening, so that, when 'Eagle Day' dawned, the defenders could again see what was happening.

From then on, the pressure on Fighter Command was unremitting. The Luftwaffe no longer waited to draw the fighters into combat. They attacked them on their own airfields, or, if they were already in the air, their fields were attacked behind their backs, so that they had nowhere to land. At Tangmere, near Chichester, a pilot returning from a sortie in his Hurricane found the airfield under attack. He was obviously having great difficulty in finding a path for his landing, but he managed to touch down safely, and the aircraft rolled to a halt. Immediately it was set upon by a swarm of

enemy aircraft, guns blazing, and within seconds the Hurricane was an inferno. The ground crews made superhuman efforts to extract the pilot from his cockpit, and he was carried to hospital with severe burns. The next day he died of his injuries, and Pilot Officer William Fiske became the first American volunteer to die flying with the RAF in the defence of Great Britain.

It was on the same day that the Victoria Cross – Britains highest award for gallantry in combat – was awarded to Flight Lieutenant James Nicolson. Nicolson was leading a flight of three Hurricanes into an attack on a formation of Bf.110s, when the Hurricanes themselves were attacked by Bf.109s diving out of the sun. Immediately all three Hurricanes were hit, two of them bursting into flames. As his wing man abandoned his blazing aircraft, Nicolson, wounded by cannon shells which had struck his aircraft, and sitting in a cockpit full of flames from a ruptured fuel tank, realised that his Bf.110 was still in his sights. He remained in his aircraft to press home the attack, before he himself bailed out, suffering serious burns to his face and hands, and with his clothing alight. It was the only time that the Victoria Cross was awarded to a Fighter Command pilot in the whole of World War Two. Sadly, Nicolson was never credited with the Messerschmitt which he destroyed, and he died later in the war when an aircraft in which he was travelling as a passenger crashed.

Day after day the battle continued. Day after day the Royal Air Force destroyed two enemy aircraft for each one they lost. But their fighter pilots were under continuous strain, attacked on the ground as well as in the air, and the Luftwaffe had had more than twice as many aircraft to begin with. By the end of August Fighter Command was virtually on its knees. New pilots were coming from the training schools with less than ten hours training on front-line fighters. Bomber pilots were being transferred to fill the gaps. At this crucial moment the Luftwaffe changed its tactics.

On 24 August German bombs fell on London. It is now believed that this was accidental. A bomber, uncertain of its position and in difficulties, jettisoned its load to help make good its escape. The RAF retaliated. Over a succession of evenings Bomber Command despatched 80 aircraft or more to attack targets in Berlin. This Hitler could not tolerate. On

September 2 the Luftwaffe received orders that from now on the main target was to be London.

Five days later the new strategy was put into effect. September 7 started quietly, then towards the end of the afternoon the defenders became aware that a raid, which looked like the biggest so far, was building up. Almost a thousand enemy aircraft flew towards the Thames estuary. As they had done on previous days, the fighters fell back inland to defend their airfields, so that when the raiders turned west to follow the River Thames, they had an unopposed approach to the city of London. The fighters rushed in to protect their capital, but they were too late. The Germans lost 40 aircraft as they fought their way home, but by that time the docklands, and the residential areas of London's East End which surrounded them, were ablaze. The sky was hidden by thick, black smoke. As darkness fell it was the turn of the night bombers. Some 250 aircraft, their target illuminated by the fires which blazed under the pall of smoke, marked as no target

had ever been marked before, dropped their bombs into the inferno. Even more bombs than had fallen during the daylight raid.

London's loss was Fighter Command's gain. Now that their airfields were left alone, they were able to operate with renewed confidence and vigour, even though their resources were saturated by the concentrations of raiders thrown against them.

The climax came on September 15. Wave upon wave of raiders assembled over the French coast, watched by the far-seeing eye of the RAF's radar. A mass of aircraft which took so long to assemble that 17 of 11 Group's squadrons were able to get airborne and climb to a favourable height over the south of England while waiting for the attack to come. There was even time for five of 12 Group's squadrons to form up into their 'big wing', to back them up. Even so, it was impossible to deflect such an armada. Large numbers of the raiders reached London. Harassed by the fighters it was impossible for them to aim at specific targets.

The Home Guard, on duty again, watch over a Junkers Ju.88.

German aircraft shot down over England were a valuable source of technical intelligence, and were guarded to prevent pilfering by souvenir hunters. Home Guard soldiers, in full field order, pass the time by studying the victory symbols on the fin of a Messerschmitt Bf.110.

Haphazardly their bomb-loads rained down across London and its suburbs, before they turned for home, severely mauled. Then, as the fighters landed to refuel and rearm, more raiders approached. Air Vice-Marshal Park called for more support from his neighbours in 12 Group. Prime Minister Winston Churchill was visiting 11 Group's Headquarters at Uxbridge, and was watching the activity in the Operations Room from the gallery above. The state boards seemed to indicate that all the available squadrons in 11 Group were either engaged, or on the ground being refuelled and rearmed. 'What reserves have we?', he asked. 'There are none, sir.' replied Park. But with this last gasp the enemy was repulsed.

'185 Victories!', cried the newspapers next morning. When the claims had been checked, and duplicates had been eliminated, the true tally was nearer 60. Even so, the Luftwaffe was defeated.

The German daylight attacks on England, their attempt to overthrow the Royal Air Force and pave the way for the invasion of Britain;,showed a sharp downturn. At German War Headquarters, the War Diary recorded, 'The enemy air force is still by no means defeated. On the contrary, it shows increasing activity. The weather situation does not permit us to expect a period of calm. The Fuhrer therefore decides to postpone Operation "Sealion" indefinitely.'

The Battle of Britain had been won. The tide had been turned by 3,080 young men of 14 different nationalities, serving with the Royal Air Force. More than one in five of them died during the Battle, and less than half of them would survive to celebrate the final victory in 1945. In the words of Churchill, that great orator who, on September 15 had looked in vain for reserves: 'Never was so much owed by so many to so few.'

THE DEFENCE OF MALTA

Approached by air Malta looks like a leaf floating on the Mediterranean, green or yellow depending on the time of year. It is so small – only 142 square miles – that it is visible for a long time. It is a memorable view.

Cross the Mediterranean in any direction, and you will pass close to Malta. The island itself was, in the 1960s, turned into a holiday island by the development of mass air travel, but it had been valued for its strategic position for over 300 years.

Never was Malta's position at the hub of the Mediterranean more significant than during World War II. Italian and German forces in North Africa would need to be supplied and reinforced via the sea lanes across the Mediterranean, and so long as the British held Malta, and were free to operate from there, enemy shipping would be vulnerable.

On June 10 1940 Mussolini threw in his hand with Germany and declared war on Britain. The first task for the Italians was to open hostilities upon Malta on behalf of the Axis powers. On June 11 Malta's air raid sirens sounded for the first time.

The Royal Air Force's Hurricanes were needed either back in Britain, where the Battle of Britain was about to begin, or in North Africa to help in the fight against Rommel's Afrika Korps. Back in April it had appeared that Malta was to be left without air defence, until it was discovered that four large crates, inadvertently left behind on the quayside by the aircraft carrier H.M.S. *Glorious*, contained obsolescent biplane Gladiator fighters. The Air Officer Commanding Malta, Air Commodore F.H.M. Maynard, signalled the Admiral of the British Mediterranean Fleet for permission to use them until *Glorious* could return for them. His request was granted. One of the Gladiators was soon

Right: a Gloster Gladiator. From the first air raid on Malta, on June 11, 1940, until the end of that month, three Gladiators, 'Faith', 'Hope' and 'Charity', provided Malta's only airborne air defence - they gave such a good account of themselves that within a week the Italian bombers were appearing with a fighter escort. The first Italian fighter to appear over the island was the Macchi C.200 (below).

Cant Z 1007 bis three-engined bombers of the Regia Aeronautica locate Grand Harbour, Valetta, through a break in the clouds, and release their bomb load.

A relic of the Regia
Aeronautica. Over
1,100 Italian and
German aircraft were
shot down by Malta's
defences. With less
than 150 square miles
upon which they
could fall, sights such
as this were
commonplace.

damaged on the ground, so, by the time the Regia Aeronautica arrived on June 11, the remaining three, nicknamed 'Faith', 'Hope' and 'Charity', were all there was to drive away the Savoia-Marchetti S-79 bombers.

For the first week there were constant air raids. 'Faith', 'Hope' and 'Charity', hugely outnumbered, climbed from their airfield to the attack. The people stood in the streets and cheered; photographs of the pilots appeared in shop windows. They fought to such telling effect that, after a week, the Italians arrived with an escort of Macchi 200 fighters. The Air Commodore's signal back to Britain emphasised that, whilst this was a great compliment to his tiny force of fighters and their pilots, the need for Hurricanes was desperate.

Before the end of the month four Hurricanes,

landing on the island to refuel on their way to North Africa, were pressed into service. From then on the air defence of Malta was in the hands of modern fighters, although the Gladiators continued to take part. Three years later, 'Faith', the only one to have survived, was handed to the people of Malta as a memorial, and a testimony to their own valour and determination. It still stands as the proud centrepiece in Malta's War Museum. During their few weeks of glory the Gladiators had intercepted seventy-two hostile formations, and shot down or damaged thirty-seven enemy aircraft.

For two months Malta's air defense was in the hands of this scavenged handful of fighters, then, despite the pressing need for Hurricanes in Britain at the time, twelve were sent on board the aircraft carrier *Argus*. They helped the Royal

A relic of the Regia Aeronautica. Over 1,100 Italian and German aircraft were shot down by Malta's defences. With less than 150 square miles upon which they could fall, sights such as this were commonplace.

Air Force to keep control of the sky over Malta, and its bomber and reconnaissance units were able to range the Mediterranean, attacking the enemy and reporting his movements.

Despairing of the Regia Aeronautica's ability to suppress the Royal Air Force's activities from Malta, the Germans began to build up Luftwaffe units in Sicily, only seventy-five miles away. From January 1941 the Italian Savoia Marchetti S-79s were joined by Junkers Ju 87s and Ju 88s, and the Macchi 200s by Messerschmitt Bf.109s. Gradually the RAF lost its air supremacy over the island until eventually the bomber and reconnaissance aircraft could no longer operate from there, and had to be sent away to less suitable but safer bases.

In April more Hurricanes arrived. This time they were Mark IIAs, more of a match for the Bf.109s than the Mark Is. They were carried from Gibraltar on the aircraft carrier *Ark Royal* until they were within range of Malta. Then they were flown off with an escort of Fleet Air Arm Skuas to help with the navigation. Some degree of air supremacy began to be regained. More Hurricanes arrived, and soon it was possible to bring back the bombers. The Luftwaffe began to move out of Sicily. They were required in the build up for the Russian front, and by the time Malta's new Air Officer Commanding, Air Vice-Marshal Sir Hugh Pugh Lloyd, arrived in May, he found not only an effective air defence force, but one that was confronted only by the Regia Aeronautica.

For the rest of 1941 Malta's air role became

The last of Malta's Gladiators: 'Faith', 'Hope' or 'Charity'? Whichever it was, the remains were preserved until after the war, and now form the centrepiece of the island's World War II museum.

After the three Gladiators had struggled alone to defend Malta for three weeks, four Hurricanes fell into the air officer commanding's net. From then on, though the biplanes still played their part for many months, the main burden of defence rested upon the humpbacks of the Hurricanes.

largely offensive. Royal Air Force bombers and Fleet Air Arm strike aircraft attacked targets in North Africa, and shipping throughout the Mediterranean area. In their operations from April to November, they sank over 160,000 tons of enemy shipping between them, and damaged a similar amount. The Italians continued to make sporadic bombing raids against the island, including night attacks. Some of the Hurricanes were formed into a night fighting force, and established a unique technique in co-operation with the searchlight batteries for dealing with raiders. Then, in December, the Luftwaffe returned to Sicily.

Malta was again subjected to a devastating series of air raids. During February of 1942 there were almost two thousand bomber sorties against the island. In an effort to achieve complete domination of the air, the Luftwaffe flew constant fighter patrols overhead, and the Hurricanes were both outclassed and outnumbered. The RAF's bomber effort was halved. A Royal Artillery officer in the anti-aircraft batteries suggested that instead of reporting all the air raids, it would be simpler, and equally accurate, if the radio announced that 'During the last month Malta had six all clears, one of which lasted for twenty five

Left: puffballs of cumulus cloud sit upon Malta's hilltops. The Italians had expected to overwhelm the island in weeks, but by the end of 1940 there was still no sign of them succeeding. On January 16, 1941, the first German attack took place. A formation of Junkers Ju.88s (above) was escorted by Italian CR 42 fighters.

minutes'. He was not far from wrong. On one day in February the island had a record number of alerts, which totalled over thirteen hours.

Air Vice-Marshal Lloyd reported to his Commander-in-Chief that it was becoming impossible to do any work. His airfields were under almost continuous attack, and there was not time, between raids, to repair the damage to the runways. What he urgently needed was reinforcement of his Hurricanes by Spitfires. Two days later fifteen of them arrived. They came through Gibraltar, and, like the Hurricanes before them, they were brought to within range by an aircraft carrier. The Hurricanes were up to provide cover, and they

all arrived safely. The Spitfires, helped by a spell of bad weather, provided a breathing space. Work on the airfields proceeded furiously, and the gunners were able to relax for a while.

Throughout it all, it must be remembered, the convoys were bringing supplies. Food and fuel for the troops and for the civilian population, ammunition and spare parts, all had to come by sea. The Germans attacked the convoys with aircraft and submarines, and the Royal Air Force flew sorties to protect them. The aim was for a convoy each month, but the convoy for February 1942 failed completely to get anywhere near the island. In desperation aviation fuel was brought in by submarine. And

Junkers Ju.87 dive bombers (left) flown by Italian pilots had attacked Malta as early as September 1940. On January 16, 1941, a formation of Luftwaffe Stukas raided the island shortly after the Ju.88s. Their main target was the aircraft carrier HMS *Illustrious*, which was in Grand Harbour, Valetta, undergoing urgent repairs to bomb damage.

Malta had not been self-sufficient in almost 400 years as a garrison island. Urgent essential supplies were sometimes carried in a fast minelayer, HMS *Welshman*, capable of over 40 knots and able to operate alone. When things were really desperate, it was not unknown for small quantities of aircraft fuel to be brought in by submarine. But to victual the island in the quantities that were really needed, the only practical answer was the convoy (below left).

Right: aircraft handlers on the fight deck of a Royal Navy aircraft carrier position Spitfires ready to take off for the journey to Malta. These departures were an adventure for the RAF pilots, who had no training in carrier operations.

when the convoys did manage to get through they were subjected to constant attack while unloading.

As we have seen, even replacement fighter aircraft came most of the way by sea, until they were close enough to fly into the the island. On April 20, 1942 a strong force of 47 Spitfires was carried to within range by the American carrier *Wasp*. Unfortunately, the arrival of the formation was spotted by German radar seventy miles away in Sicily, and an intense air raid was mounted immediately. The new arrivals were caught on the airfields by the initial attack, and by succeeding waves of bombers. Within three days all had been destroyed. Two weeks later another sixty Spitfires were despatched by USS *Wasp* and HMS *Eagle*. Learning from their previous experience, the British this time had every available hand waiting for them. Scores of airmen, aided by soldiers and sailors, were ready to refuel and rearm them the moment they arrived. Wherever possible their pilots were replaced by men with combat experience over Malta. By the time the expected air raid

Blackburn Skua dive bombers on board HMS *Ark Royal* in the Mediterranean during 1941. The most economical way of getting fighter reinforcements to Malta was to embark them onto aircraft carriers at Gibraltar, and carry them to within their own flying range of the island.

One third of Malta, to the north, was rocky and unsuitable for airfields. Three airfields and an emergency strip were squeezed into the southern part. Takali nestled at the base of the hills, and was overlooked by the ancient towns of M'dina and Rabat.

took place the Spitfires were back in the air, defending themselves and the island, and they were successfully absorbed into the island's air defence force.

And so the battle ebbed and flowed. Day after day, month after month, the island was attacked. The defenders fought to clear the skies so that the bombers and the reconnaissance aircraft could take off to go about their business. They fought to get the shipping through, and to protect it while it was unloaded. Gradually they succeeded. By the winter of 1942 the siege was lifted.

The battle had lasted over two years, during which time an estimated 14,000 tons of bombs had fallen on the island. That was more than ninety-five tons on each square mile. Some 1,500 civilians had been killed or had died of injuries and about 25,000 buildings had been destroyed or damaged. There had been terror. There had been half rations, for serviceman and civilian alike. There had been disease, and all the after effects of undernourishment. But from this battle Malta emerged to dominate the central Mediterranean as a striking base. Britain has an award – the George Cross – named after its patron saint, St George. It is the highest award for bravery that can be made to a civilian. King George VI announced, 'To HONOUR HER BRAVE PEOPLE I AWARD THE GEORGE CROSS TO THE ISLAND FORTRESS OF MALTA TO BEAR WITNESS TO A HEROISM AND DEVOTION THAT WILL LONG BE FAMOUS IN HISTORY.'

BATTLE OF TARANTO

A naval capital ship – battleship or battlecruiser – is able to exert tremendous influence on a theatre of war without actually doing anything. It poses such a threat that, even when it is lying in port, its opponents must dedicate significant forces to ensure that it stays there, or to provide immediate intelligence should it leave. Although a whole fleet need not be tied up in this operation, nevertheless its freedom of action is drastically curtailed. It dare not roam too far afield, in case the quarry should break out whilst its back is turned. This was precisely the problem which confronted Admiral Sir Andrew Cunningham, Commander-in-Chief of the British Mediterranean Fleet in May 1940, as a result of Italy entering the war on the side of Germany. Previously Cunningham had had the Mediterranean more or less to himself. Now he had a major hostile fleet to keep his eye on,

a fleet which included at least half a dozen battleships.

The Italian fleet had established itself at Taranto, in the 'arch' of the foot of Italy, and seemed less enthusiastic than Cunningham to have the showdown. Cunningham needed the showdown, to enable him to recover the freedom that he had enjoyed before May. Rear-Admiral A.L.St G. Lyster, commanding Cunningham's carrier group wrote, 'They show no inclination to venture far from the Gulf of Taranto, and since it is difficult to find any inducement to make them do so, you must consider an air attack in the harbour'. The prospect of the need to attack Taranto had been predicted as long ago as 1938, when Lyster, then Captain of the ill-fated HMS *Glorious*, had been asked to devise a plan for such an attack, and to train his crews accordingly.

It was essential to keep a close watch (left) on the Italian warships assembled in Taranto. As the Royal Air Force gained some command of the air over Malta, their reconnaissance aircraft, both land-based aircraft and seaplanes, were able to assist the aircraft of the Fleet Air Arm to monitor the comings and goings of the Italians.

On June 11, 1940, Italy entered World War II alongside Germany. One of the immediate effects of this was to alter the balance of the naval war in the Mediterranean. Some months before the Italian declaration of war, Italy's fleet (right) assembles for a review in the Bay of Naples.

Up until the very day that the Fleet Air Arm launched their attack against Taranto from the aircraft carrier HMS *Illustrious*, RAF Sunderlands (left) brought back photographs showing where the Italian ships lay in the two basins of the harbor.

Right: the deck landing control officer guides a Swordfish back onto the flight deck of an aircraft carrier. The aircraft's arrester hook is deployed to catch on one of the wires stretched across the deck beside the officer.

Glorious, alas, was no more, but many of the crews Lyster had trained two years earlier were now in HMS *Illustrious* in the Mediterranean.

There were certain requirements before the attack could proceed. Not least was the need for up to date reconnaissance. This was to confirm that the Italian battleships and cruisers were still in Taranto, and, far more important, to show exactly where they were berthed. The harbour was extensive, with an inner harbour, the Mar Piccolo, and the outer Mar Grande. The aircraft would need to know just where they were going. In a night attack, in the face of the enemy defences, they would not want to have to go looking for their targets.

To enable the attack to be launched from outside the radius of the normal Italian reconnaissance, the aircraft would have to be fitted with long-range fuel tanks. To make room for the extra tanks they were going to have to fly without their telegraphist/gunner. And the pilots and observers would need special night

flying training before being despatched on a hazardous long distance night flight.

The raid was intended to be carried out on October 21, but at that time the fleet was required to cover important convoy movements. It was rescheduled for the night of November 11. It had been intended that HMS *Eagle* would combine with *Illustrious* for the operation, but she had suffered damage from Italian dive-bombers during the convoy work, and repairs were not complete. Five of her Swordfish aircraft were embarked in *Illustrious*, to make up the numbers.

For several days before the operation was due to take place the Royal Air Force from Malta flew a series of reconnaissances over the Italian port. Their Sunderland flying-boats and American-built Glen Marylands defied the anti-aircraft fire and the Italian fighters, to bring back the vital information, and supporting photographs. They showed that the fleet in Taranto included five battleships, fourteen

cruisers and twenty-seven destroyers. An aircraft from the carrier flew to Malta to collect the photographs needed for briefing the Swordfish crews. During November 11 the RAF had another look at Taranto, to make sure that nothing had changed. They were able to report that the only change was the arrival of a sixth battleship. The scene was set.

At 6 p.m. *Illustrious*, with an escort of four cruisers and four destroyers, detached from the fleet, and set course for the flying-off point, 170 miles from Taranto. Once there, the first strike of twelve Swordfish was ranged on deck. The RAF's photographs had indicated the extent of barrage balloons and torpedo nets around the target, which was going to restrict the space available for torpedo attacks. Accordingly, only six of the aircraft carried 1,500lb torpedoes. Two carried a combination of bombs and flares, and the remaining four carried a load consisting entirely of bombs.

Just before 9 p.m. they took off, formed up, and set off for Taranto at their leisurely cruising speed of around 100 mph. With their two-man crews in their open cockpits, the fixed undercarriage biplanes looked more like relics of World War I. The torpedo carriers were to attack the battleships, moored in the Mar Grande, the outer harbour, while the others were to head for the cruisers and destroyers along the quayside in the Mar Piccolo.

At approximately 11 p.m. the flare-carrying aircraft separated from their colleagues to carry out their task of illuminating the harbour. Flares were laid along the east side of the harbour, silhouetting their targets for the others, and the flare droppers then went on to carry out dive-bomb attacks on the harbour installations, setting the fuel storage tanks on fire.

In the light of the flares the first flight of three torpedo aircraft swept over the Mar Grande, heading for the battleships. Halfway across, the leader disappeared, and was not seen again. Number two came down to within 30

The ungainly Supermarine Walrus amphibian was, surprisingly, a product of the same drawing board as the elegant Spitfire. With wings which folded back alongside its fuselage, the Walrus could be carried in a hangar built between the funnels of the British battleships and cruisers. It performed invaluable service as 'the eyes of the fleet', and rescued many Fleet Air Arm aircrew who had failed to return their carrier.

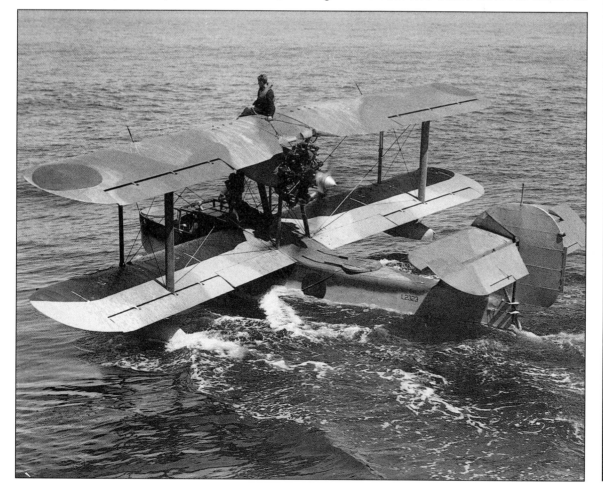

The British Mediterranean Fleet was hampered by the presence of the battleship *Conte di Cavour* (above), and other elements of the Italian fleet, sheltering in Taranto. Although apparently loath to confront Admiral Cunningham's fleet, the Italian ships were a threat that stopped him moving freely.

feet of the water, and launched his torpedo from 700 yards. Hauling the aircraft round, the pilot weaved through intense flak. As he crossed the breakwater, heading back out to sea, he heard a huge explosion behind him. The third Swordfish of the flight attacked the same target, and the second formation of three selected other battleships as targets. All reported hits. By this time the cruisers and destroyers in the Mar Piccolo had opened fire, but their shells seemed to be a greater danger to the merchant ships in the Mar Grande than to the Swordfish, and some of the barrage balloons were hit and set

on fire. Meanwhile, the remaining aircraft carried out successful attacks in the inner harbour, except for one which could not find a suitable target amidst the smoke, and instead attacked the seaplane base just along the coast, setting fire to a hangar. All the aircraft returned to the carrier, except the one which had disappeared on the first run in.

A second strike of nine Swordfish flew off from *Illustrious* twenty-five minutes after the first. Five carried torpedoes, two carried bombs and the remaining two a mixture of bombs and flares. One aircraft was damaged in a

With a maximum speed of 139 mph, and a somewhat lower cruising speed, the Swordfish crew (left) had plenty of time to look around them, and to contemplate what lay ahead.

Below left: diving almost to wave-top height, a Fleet Air Arm Swordfish launches its torpedo.

Perched high above the flight deck in the exposed cockpits of their Fairey Swordfish, the pilot and observer of this Fleet Air Arm aircraft receive last-minute intelligence. The Swordfish normally carried a third crew member, a telegraphist/airgunner, but they were left behind for the Taranto raid to enable the aircraft to carry extra fuel.

collision on the deck, and could not take off. He was allowed to follow the formation twenty minutes later, after running repairs had been carried out. The observer was having an eventful day. In the morning he had been in an aircraft which had force landed twenty miles from the carrier, and had been thrown into the sea. A rescuing cruiser had returned him to his ship in its Walrus float-plane.

While still sixty miles from the target, the second wave could see the fires started by the aircraft which had already attacked. At midnight they began to make their own attacks, again the torpedo aircraft heading for the battleships and the bombers making for the quaysides. By now shore batteries, cruisers and battleships were all in action, but several of the Swordfish crews reported that the cruisers still seemed to be hitting the merchant ships, and now the battleships were hitting the cruisers.

By the time the late arrival got to the scene, everyone else was on the way home, and the entire defences of Taranto were able to concentrate on him. Somehow he managed to weave through the flak, unload his bombs on the cruisers and head for home behind the

others. Only two Swordfish failed to return – one from each wave. Of their crews, one was killed and three taken prisoner. As one of the pilots said, 'Only the Swordfish, with its ability to twist and turn, could have got through that fire.' They may have referred to their pedestrian biplane as 'the old string-bag', but they had great respect for it. Taranto was not the only battle during World War II in which it was to distinguish itself. A contemporary magazine quipped,

'Lots of struts in all directions,
Curved and cut-out centre sections.
"Stringbag"-the-Sailor's had his day,
But in his own distinguished way
He's left his mark on history's page,
A relic of the biplane age.'

The next day the RAF returned to Taranto to take some more pictures. They showed that, for the time being, Admiral Cunningham would no longer have to watch what was happening behind his back. Three of the battleships had been sunk, as had two auxiliaries. Two of the cruisers were listing heavily and were surrounded by fuel oil, and the oil tanks and the seaplane base had been damaged. *Illustrious*

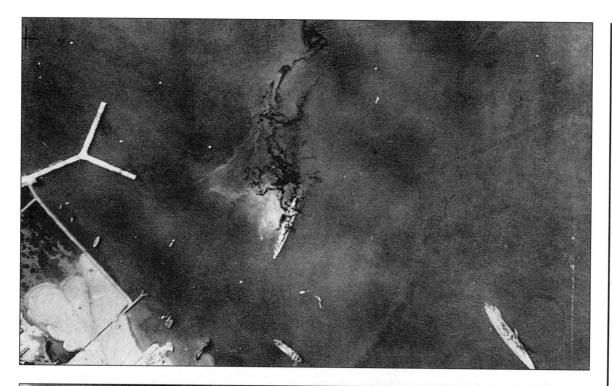

RAF reconnaissance aircraft returned to Taranto after the attack, and came back with dramatic photographs of the result. Left: in the inner harbour, two Trento-class cruisers, and one of the Belzano class, lie amidst the oil slick seeping from their ruptured fuel tanks.

Below left: in the outer harbour, the Mare Grande, reconnaissance showed the battleship *Littorio* lying with a heavy list and her fo'c'sle awash, and a Cavour-class battleship with her stern underwater as far as the after gun turret.

Below: a Swordfish takes off from HMS *Ark Royal*. An aircraft carrier steaming ahead created a wind along the flight deck which enabled the Swordfish to take off without the aid of a catapult.

and her group rejoined the fleet. As they did so their Admiral greeted them with a brief standard fleet signal – 'Manoeuvre well carried out.'

Winston Churchill, in Britain, wrote to President Roosevelt, 'I am sure you will be pleased about Taranto. The three remaining battleships have now left Taranto; perhaps they are withdrawing to Trieste.'

Churchill himself was to comment that, by a touch of irony, on the very day that the Mediterranean fleet attacked Taranto, an Italian bomber force escorted by sixty fighters attacked Britain. Eight of the bombers and five fighters were shot down. 'They might have found better employment,' suggested Churchill, 'defending their fleet at Taranto.'

Taranto was the first decisive strike by carrier-borne aircraft of World War II.

INFAMY AT PEARL HARBOR

There have been times in history when a battle has become better remembered for the disreputable actions of the diplomats which led up to it than for the brilliant execution of the military action. This is very much the case with the 'day of infamy', as President Franklin D. Roosevelt called it, at Pearl Harbor on December 7, 1941. The infamy was a combination of deceit and inefficiency on the part of the Japanese diplomatic corps. Viewed with the detachment which is possible half a century later, the attack itself can be seen as a brilliantly executed military operation.

Throughout the 1930s the Japanese had been waging war against China. Their desire to expand economically required parallel territorial expansion, and China was an obvious target. By 1940 other factors were becoming involved. America was starving them of fuel supplies, so Japan began to look towards Indonesia as a source. The Indonesian oil fields were under the the control of the Dutch. As a result of American influence, Japanese negotiations with the Dutch for the supply of fuel broke down. The only recourse was conquest, but America could not be expected to stand idly by while Japan invaded Indonesia. The first task, then, was to strike at America, so that she would be impotent to interfere. The best way to ensure success was to strike without warning, or, at least, without sufficient warning for America to prepare herself. In the event, the

This photograph of a model of 'Battleship Row', at Pearl Harbor, was discovered in Japan after the war. Was it created as a target model, or simply as a tourist attraction?

Right: the 'Zero'. The Mitsubishi A6M Zero-Sen, code-named 'Zeke' in the official American aircraft recognition books, became universally known and feared as the 'Zero' during the first year of the Pacific War. Until Pearl Harbor, the United States Navy was not aware of by how much the 'Zero' outclassed their best fighters.

Six Japanese aircraft carriers (below right) headed towards the flying-off point, 200 miles north of Honolulu, to launch the attack on Pearl Harbor. Between them they carried over 400 combat aircraft.

strike did take place without any warning at all, due to the inefficiency of the staff of the Japanese Embassy in Washington, who failed to decode the ciphered declaration of war in time to deliver it by the appointed hour.

As well as the element of surprise, a significant factor in the Japanese success was the training and experience of their aircrews. Just as the Germans had taken the opportunities of the Spanish Civil War to perfect and practice their techniques, the Japanese had the benefit of ten years fighting in China. This was no untried force, depending on the pure theory of their training manuals, which was about to be unleashed on the American forces in the Pacific.

The objective was to immobilise the American fleet as it lay at Pearl Harbor. Pearl Harbor lies near Honolulu, on Oahu, one of the islands in the Hawaiian group. In particular Japan hoped to clip the wings of the American fleet by destroying its aircraft carriers.

The majority of the Imperial Japanese Naval Air Force was to be allocated to the task. The Task Force included six aircraft carriers. Two of them, the *Zuikaku*, and the *Shokaku*, were less than one year old. The six carriers, between them, carried over four hundred aircraft. Those to be used were the Nakajima B5N 'Kate', which would be used as a conventional bomber, and as a low level torpedo bomber;

The carrier USS *Lexington* was one of the prime targets in the attack on Pearl Harbor. Luckily, when the Japanese struck, the *Lexington* was at sea, delivering reinforcements of aircraft to the American base at Midway Island. Her luck was short-lived. The 'Kates' caught up with her five months later at the Battle of the Coral Sea.

The Nakajima B5N2 'Kate' was the best Japanese carrier-based torpedo bomber until 1944. The Japanese fleet launched 144 'Kates' to take part in the attack on Pearl Harbor.

Overleaf, left: one of the most spectacular photographs of the attack on Pearl Harbor was taken at the moment when the magazine of the destroyer USS *Shaw* exploded. Looking at the photograph, it does not seem possible that the *Shaw* was able to be repaired and returned to active service.

Overleaf, right: American sailors struggle to salvage what they can of their aircraft at the naval air base on Ford Island. In the background, a fuel storage tank erupts as it is hit by a bomb from the second wave of Japanese bombers.

the fixed-undercarriage Aichi D3A 'Val', in skilled hands an effective dive bomber, and as fighter escort; and for ground strafing, the Mitsubishi A6M Zero-Sen. Officially code named 'Zeke', the A6M was to become known, and universally feared, as the 'Zero'.

The six carriers were supported by two battleships, three cruisers, nine destroyers, and an eight ship replenishment group. The fleet, commanded by Vice-Admiral Chuichi Nagumo, sailed surreptitiously from Japan on November 26, 1941, and covered 3,000 miles to a point approximately 250 miles north of Pearl Harbor by Sunday, December 7.

Almost one hundred warships waited unsuspectingly in Pearl Harbor for the Japanese attack, but not a single aircraft carrier. The *Enterprise* and the *Lexington* were at sea, delivering aircraft to strengthen the garrisons at Wake and Midway. The prizes which the Japanese most desperately wanted were out of harm's way.

Before first light on April 7 the decks of

Nagumo's carriers came alive with activity, as the 214 aircraft of the first strike were prepared for takeoff. Off duty personnel were encouraged on deck to cheer as the first aircraft took off into the dawn and circled the fleet waiting for the rest of the formations to join them. At approximately the same time that the Japanese Declaration of War should have been being handed to the American Government, the 'Kates', 'Vals' and 'Zeros' set course for Hawaii. Two hours later, as the United States Navy on Oahu were about to go to breakfast, they arrived over their target. The Zero's weaved above the formations of bombers, ready to deal with any interference, but none came.

Two army radar operators in the north of the island picked up the echo of what was, in fact, a Japanese float plane scouting ahead of the formation. But it was a beautiful Sunday morning, America was not at war, and this was most likely a private pilot, up for a lesson before the heat of the day. Neither of the operators, nor the officer to whom they reported their

contact, were concerned. A little later, the screen came alive again. This time it indicated so many aircraft, approaching from about 150 miles range, that anyone would sit up and take notice. Again the duty officer at the plotting centre was not alarmed. A formation of B-17s were due to be delivered that morning, from California. Maybe this was them. And *Enterprise* was expected back from Wake Island. She could very well have sent some of her aircraft on ahead.

As the Japanese torpedo bombers began their run in, the dive bombers hurtled past them to fling their deadly loads at the massed warships in the harbour. Elsewhere on the island other formations were attacking the airfields and military installations, while the Zeros, with no defending fighters to occupy them, turned their attentions to targets of opportunity on the ground.

Response from the ground was slow to appear. In a military force in peacetime it is a most terrible crime to lose ammunition, or to fire it without authority. Most ammunition on Oahu, therefore, was under lock and key, and those who did have any had first to overcome their

The wreckage of a Chance-Vought OS2U Kingfisher float plane. Over eighty American aircraft were destroyed during the Japanese attack.

Immediately after the attack, the battleship USS *Tennessee* moved into one of the docks at Pearl Harbor for emergency repairs that would enable her to return to a dockyard on the west coast of America. She was back in service with the fleet by May 1942. In front of her in the dock is a badly damaged destroyer.

Honolulu Star-Bulletin 1st EXTRA

8 PAGES—HONOLULU, TERRITORY OF HAWAII, U. S. A., SUNDAY, DECEMBER 7, 1941—8 PAGES ★ PRICE FIVE CENTS

WAR!

(Associated Press by Transpacific Telephone)

SAN FRANCISCO, Dec. 7.— President Roosevelt announced this morning that Japanese planes had attacked Manila and Pearl Harbor.

OAHU BOMBED BY JAPANESE PLANES

SIX KNOWN DEAD, 21 INJURED, AT EMERGENCY HOSPITAL

Attack Made On Island's Defense Areas

By UNITED PRESS

WASHINGTON, Dec. 7.—Text of a White House announcement detailing the attack on the Hawaiian islands is:

"The Japanese attacked Pearl Harbor from the air and all naval and military activities on the island of Oahu, principal American base in the Hawaiian islands."

Oahu was attacked at 7:55 this morning by Japanese planes.

The Rising Sun, emblem of Japan, was seen on plane wing tips.

Wave after wave of bombers streamed through the clouded morning sky from the southwest and flung their missiles on a city resting in peaceful Sabbath calm.

According to an unconfirmed report received at the governor's office, the Japanese force that attacked Oahu reached island waters aboard two small airplane carriers.

It was also reported that at the governor's office either an attempt had been made to bomb the USS Lexington, or that it had been bombed.

CITY IN UPROAR

Within 10 minutes the city was in an uproar. As bombs fell in many parts of the city, and in defense areas the defenders of the islands went into quick action.

Army intelligence officers at Ft. Shafter announced officially shortly after 9 a. m. the fact of the bombardment by an enemy but long previous army and navy had taken immediate measures in defense.

"Oahu is under a sporadic air raid," the announcement said.

"Civilians are ordered to stay off the streets until further notice."

CIVILIANS ORDERED OFF STREETS

The army has ordered that all civilians stay off the streets and highways and not use telephones.

Evidence that the Japanese attack has registered some hits was shown by three billowing pillars of smoke in the Pearl Harbor and Hickam field area.

All navy personnel and civilian defense workers, with the exception of women, have been ordered to duty at Pearl Harbor.

The Pearl Harbor highway was immediately a mass of racing cars.

A trickling stream of injured people began pouring into the city emergency hospital a few minutes after the bombardment started.

Thousands of telephone calls almost swamped the Mutual Telephone Co., which put extra operators on duty.

At The Star-Bulletin office the phone calls deluged the single operator and it was impossible for this newspaper, for sometime, to handle the flood of calls. Here also an emergency operator was called.

HOUR OF ATTACK 7:55 A. M.

An official army report from department headquarters, made public shortly before 11, is that the first attack was at 7:55 a. m.

Witnesses said they saw at least 50 airplanes over Pearl Harbor.

The attack centered in the Pearl Harbor, Army authorities said:

"The rising sun was seen on the wing tips of the airplanes."

Although martial law has not been declared officially, the city of Honolulu was operating under M-Day conditions.

It is reliably reported that enemy objectives under attack were Wheeler field Hickam field, Kaneohe bay and naval air station and Pearl Harbor.

Some enemy planes were reported shot down.

The body of the pilot was seen in a plane burning at Wahiawa.

Oahu appeared to be taking calmly after the first uproar of queries.

ANTIAIRCRAFT GUNS IN ACTION

First indication of the raid came shortly before 8 this morning when antiaircraft guns around Pearl Harbor began sending up a thunderous barrage.

At the same time a vast cloud of black smoke arose from the naval base and also from Hickam field where flames could be seen.

BOMB NEAR GOVERNOR'S MANSION

Shortly before 9:30 a bomb fell near Washington Place, the residence of the governor. Governor Poindexter and Secretary Charles M. Hite were there.

It was reported that the bomb killed an unidentified Chinese man across the street in front of the Schuman Carriage Co. where windows were broken.

C. E. Daniels, a welder, found a fragment of shell or bomb at South and Queen Sts. which he brought into the City Hall. This fragment weighed about a pound.

At 10:05 a. m. today Governor Poindexter telephoned to The Star-Bulletin announcing he has declared a state of emergency for the entire territory.

He announced that Edouard L. Doty, executive secretary of the major disaster council, has been appointed director under the M-Day law's provisions.

Governor Poindexter urged all residents of Honolulu to remain off the street, and the people of the territory to remain calm.

Mr. Doty reported that all major disaster council wardens and medical units were on duty within a half hour of the time the alarm was given.

Workers employed at Pearl Harbor were ordered at 10:10 a. m. not to report at Pearl Harbor.

The mayor's major disaster council was to meet at the city hall at about 10:30 this morning.

At least two Japanese planes were reported at Hawaiian department headquarters to have been shot down.

One of the planes was shot down at Ft. Kamehameha and the other back of the Wa-

Turn to Page 2, Column 1

Hundreds See City Bombed

Hundreds of Honolulans who hurried to the top of Punchbowl soon after bombs began to fall, saw spread out before them the whole panorama of surprise attack and defense.

Far off over Pearl Harbor the white sky was polka-dotted with anti-aircraft smoke.

Rolling away from the navy base were billowing clouds of ugly black smoke. Sometimes a burst of flame reddened the black sources of the smoke.

Out from the river-surfaced mouth of the harbor a flotilla of destroyers streamed in battle, smoke pouring from their stacks.

Turn to Page 2, Column 2

Schools Closed

All schools on Oahu, both public and private, will remain closed until further notice, Edouard L. Doty, territorial director of civilian defense, announced at 11 a. m. today. This does not apply elsewhere in the territory.

Names of Dead and Injured

The city emergency hospital reported at 10:30 a list of 6 killed and 21 injured.

The complete list will be carried later. Here is a partial list:

Peter Lopez, 34, of 3641 Kamanaiki St., was reported at 9:30 a. m. to be in serious condition from wounds in the upper abdomen.

Bernice Gouveia, 17, 2766 Kalihi St., is suffering from a mangled thigh, lacerations on the right leg and left arm.

A Portuguese girl, unidentified, 10 years old, died on arrival from puncture wounds.

Another victim who died on arrival was Frank Ohashi, 29, 2766 Kamanaiki St., from puncture wounds in the chest.

Cecilia Broadly, 33, Moanalua gardens, was released from the hospital after treatment for lacerations.

Three were reported injured and one reported killed from the bomb that fell at Fort and School Sts.

Editorial

HAWAII MEETS THE CRISIS

Honolulu and Hawaii will meet the emergency of war today as Honolulu and Hawaii have met emergencies in the past coolly, calmly and with immediate and complete support of the officials, officers and troops who are in charge.

Governor Poindexter and the army and navy leaders have called upon the public to remain calm, for civilians who have no essential business on the streets to stay off, and for every man and woman to do his duty.

That request, coupled with the measures promptly taken to meet the situation that has suddenly and terribly developed, will be needed.

Hawaii will do its part as a loyal American territory. In this crisis, every difference of race, creed and color will be submerged in the one desire and determination to play the part that Americans always play in crisis.

BULLETIN

Additional Star-Bulletin extras today will cover the latest developments in this war move.

Left: a '1st Extra' edition of the *Honolulu Star-Bulletin* of December 7, 1941, reporting the morning's air attack.

Below: the wreckage of a Japanese plane. Less than one in ten Japanese aircraft failed to return after the raid on Pearl Harbor, so that, in terms of aircraft alone, the attackers achieved a two to one advantage.

disbelief that this was really happening before opening fire.

It was not until the first wave of attackers had turned for home, and the second wave, another 170 aircraft, swept over the island, that any significant resistance was offered. Even then, the attackers had practically everything their own way.

The *Enterprise*, 200 miles out, had overheard the excited chatter on the radio during the attacks by the first wave of Japanese, and had launched aircraft to help, and to look for the hostile aircraft carriers. They arrived while the second Japanese wave was in action. At last the jubilant Zeros had the chance to do the job they had come for. By now anything that flew over Oahu was 'hostile', and a number of *Enterprise's* aircraft that were not hit by the Zeros were shot down by American gunners who did not intend to be caught napping twice in one day.

Less than two hours after the first Japanese aircraft appeared over Pearl Harbor, the sky was clear again. Clear, that is, of planes. Over Pearl Harbor, Honolulu and most of the island of Oahu, the sky was obscured by a pall of black smoke. Black smoke from burning ships, and all the other fires that had been started by the raiding formations. As they made their way back to their carriers, the attackers left behind them devastation. None of the battleships had escaped. Three were sunk; one, which had

managed to get under way during the attack, had run aground, and the rest were damaged. Three cruisers were badly damaged, two destroyers sunk and one severely damaged, and other vessels were either sunk or damaged. On the island's airfields aircraft were either destroyed or damaged. Almost 2,500 American servicemen were killed, and well over 1,000 were injured. The Japanese lost less than 30 aircraft, and about 55 men. As a military operation it was a triumph.

The major, far-reaching effect of Pearl Harbor, was that this was the incident that made World War II truly a world war. Winston Churchill, Prime Minister of Britain, had promised President Roosevelt that if war were to break out between America and Japan, Britain would declare war on Japan within two hours. He kept his word. Germany declared war on America the next day, and the echos of Pearl Harbor were heard in every corner of the world. The mastery of the Pacific had, for the time being, passed into Japanese hands, and the strategic balance of the world had changed. But Churchill rejoiced. In his view, this was the day on which the war was won. For seventeen months, since Dunkirk and the fall of France, Britain had fought alone. He records, 'No man could tell how long the war would last, nor did I at this moment care. Our history would not, after all, come to an end. United we could subdue everybody else in the world. Many disasters, immeasurable cost and tribulation lay ahead, but there was no more doubt about the end.'

The American Constitution required that the decision to declare war on Japan should be ratified by Congress. It was not until December 22 that the resolution was brought to President Roosevelt for his signature.

The Japanese could have devised no better way than their attack on Pearl Harbor of ensuring that the American population would be wholeheartedly behind the U.S. Government in their declaration of war.

THE RISING SUN

While the carrier-borne aircraft of the Japanese Navy were changing the course of history at Pearl Harbor, their land-based counterparts were far from inactive elsewhere in the Far East.

The Japanese launched a seaborne assault on the British territory of Malaya at Kota Bharu, in the northeast corner of the peninsula. All the available aircraft of the Royal Air Force and the Royal Australian Air Force were employed in an attempt to hurl the attackers back into the sea. Many sorties were flown, and significant impact was made on the landings, but it turned out that this invasion was, at the outset, more in the way of a diversion. Everything appeared to be happening at Kota Bharu, with the result that all the available defending aircraft were lured to the area. Meanwhile, the bulk of the invasion fleet was making unopposed landings fifty

miles further north, at Patani and Singora in Thailand.

This was discovered by a Beaufort of the Royal Air Force, which returned, badly damaged, from a reconnaissance of the area. The pilot reported a large concentration of Japanese vessels in the area, but, more ominously, the film from his cameras revealed that sixty or more Japanese aircraft, mostly fighters, had occupied the airfield at Singora.

The next day, the Allied air strength in the area began to wilt. The Japanese landings had carried them to the boundary of the RAF's airfield at Kota Bharu, and the ground crews were obliged to engage in hand-to-hand fighting to gain time for the aircraft – American-built Hudsons of the Australians, and obsolescent Wildebeest biplanes – to withdraw

Whilst the Japanese carrier-based aircraft were acting with such devastating effect at Pearl Harbor, their land-based counterparts of the Army Air Force were having an almost comparable influence around the Malay Peninsular. The workhorse of their fleet was the Mitsubishi Ki-21 'Sally'. Over 2,000 'Sallys' were built, and they took part in every one of Japan's major land operations.

The American-built Lockheed Hudson (right) of the Royal Australian Air Force, based at Kota Bharu, was one of the more up-to-date aircraft available to the Allies at the time of the outbreak of war in the Far East.

There was only one Bristol Beaufort (below right) operating in Malaya in December 1941. It was badly damaged on the first day of the war with Japan, as its crew obtained the vital information that Japanese troops had made a virtually unopposed landing at Singora, just one hundred miles north of the Siam/Malay border.

Practically touching the wave tops, Mitsubishi G4M 'Betty' torpedo bombers (overleaf) head for their target through a hail of anti-aircraft fire.

to Kuantan, further south. The airmen themselves were able to withdraw under cover of darkness, and escaped by train to Singapore.

While this was happening, the Japanese aircraft from Singora made heavy and continuous attacks on all the airfields in northern Malaya. It was noticed that the heaviest raids seemed to be made as the defending aircraft were landing, or being refuelled, and evidence was obtained that information on aircraft movements was being passed to the enemy. It was a disastrous day for the Allied air forces. By the evening, out of 110 aircraft available for operations in the morning, only 50 remained serviceable in the evening.

The implications of this loss of air power in northern Malaya was to be far reaching. The Royal Navy had two capital ships in the area, the latest of Britain's battleships, HMS *Prince of Wales*, accompanied by an older battlecruiser, HMS *Repulse*. With their escort of four destroyers, they had sailed from Singapore to interfere with the Japanese invasion ships at Singora. Admiral Sir Tom Phillips' little fleet had reached the area abeam Kota Bharu when he received a signal telling him that, because of the enemy air action in the area, he could no longer expect to pick up fighter cover from the local airfields. Without this fighter cover his operation at Singora would have been suicide, so he

This picture may have been taken for propaganda purposes, but there was indeed every reason for the morale of the Japanese Army Air Force pilots to be high during December 1941.

HMS *Repulse* was the older of two capital ships sent to join the Royal Navy's Far East Fleet. Commanded by Admiral Sir Tom Phillips, from HMS *Prince of Wales*, the fleet set out to harry the Japanese invasion fleets. With the loss of the RAF's airfields in northern Malaya, the fleet was soon beyond the range of effective air cover.

turned south again. On his way south he intercepted a message saying that Japanese landings were now taking place at Kuantan, and he turned to assist. The fleet was maintaining radio silence, but the Admiral assumed that his intentions would be guessed by those ashore, who would despatch air cover for him from Kuantan. In this he was wrong. His air cover never appeared, and, arriving at Kuantan to find no sign of a Japanese landing, he turned again for Singapore. Unfortunately, the delay caused by his diversion resulted in the fleet being intercepted by a force of almost 80 Japanese Navy aircraft, carrying bombs and torpedoes, who were on their way back to

their base at Saigon.

The Japanese high-level bombers achieved several near misses on the two capital ships, and then *Repulse* received a direct hit amidships. Meanwhile, the torpedo aircraft were running in, attacking in massed formation, and from either side at the same time, to make adequate defence impossible. Admiral Phillips had always maintained that a ship such as *Prince of Wales* could put up 'such a hail of steel' that no aircraft could get through. *Prince of Wales* put up a hail of steel, but to no effect. By the time the Brewster Buffalo fighters could get to the scene from Singapore, in response to a desperate signal that the fleet was under air

As HMS *Repulse* closed to help the *Prince of Wales*, she was attacked simultaneously from either side by the torpedo bombers. The use of her main armament might have been impressive, but the rate of fire of the massive fifteen-inch guns could have done little more than provide something of a smoke screen to impede the 'Bettys'. Struck by at least five torpedoes, the *Repulse* listed heavily, and sank within six minutes.

With a complete lack of air support, any success by the British gunners could provide no more than a spectacular interlude before they were overwhelmed (right) by the attacking aircraft.

The crew of the *Prince of Wales* were luckier than their colleagues in the *Repulse*. The former's more modern construction enabled her to stay afloat for almost an hour after taking three torpedoes. 1,285 officers and men (below right) were taken aboard the destroyers of the escort screen, before the *Prince of Wales* turned over and sank.

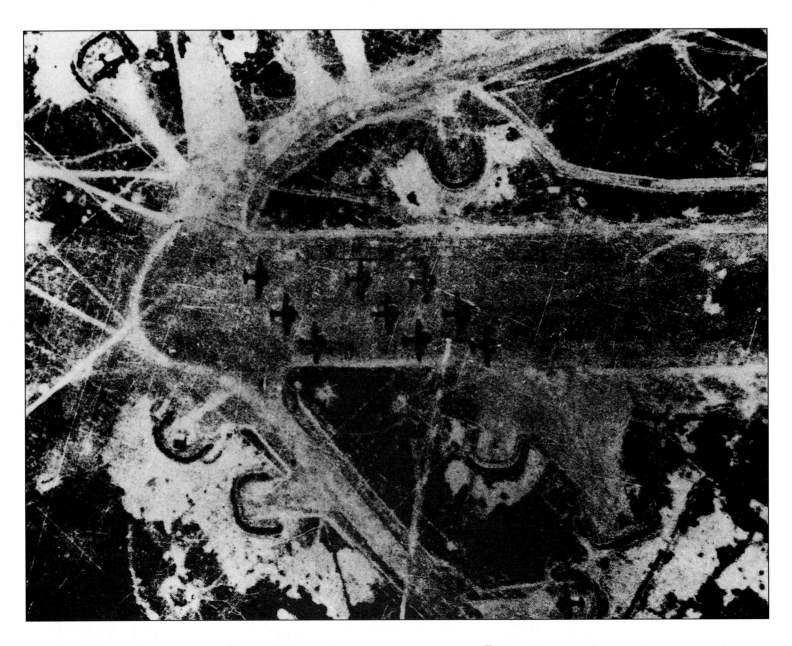

attack, it was too late. When they arrived all that was to be seen was a vast area covered with fuel oil and debris, with the destroyers moving slowly through it to pick up survivors.

This was the first time that capital ships, at sea, had been lost to air attack. From the two ships 840 officers and men were lost, including the Admiral.

After the fall of Singapore, the remains of the British Eastern Fleet was moved to Ceylon, so that, principally as a result of two tremendously successful aircraft-versus-ship actions – at Pearl Harbor and off the coast of Malaya – the Allies had, for the time being, no significant presence in the Pacific, the China Sea or the Indian Ocean. Between December 1941 and May 1942, Japan had gained control of one third of the earth's surface; an area which included the oilfields of Borneo and Indonesia, and almost 90 per cent of the world's rubber production. From the shores of Japan itself, in the north, to Australia in the south – from the Philippines in the east, to India in the west.

The conquest had taken little over four months – it would take the Allies four years to win it back.

Mitsubishi Ki-21 'Sallys' took off from their bases in Cochin, China, and ranged the South China Sea to find and bomb the British fleet. Initial bombing attacks disabled HMS *Prince of Wales*, preventing her from taking action to avoid subsequent attacks by torpedo-carrying aircraft.

THE DOOLITTLE RAID

Lieutenant Colonel 'Jimmy' Doolittle - air racer, barnstormer, and master aviator - was selected by Lieutenant General H. H. Arnold, commanding general of the United States Army Air Force, to carry out the imaginative and daring plan suggested to him by the naval aviators.

The people of the United States of America were, understandably, keen for some form of retaliation for the 'day of infamy' at Pearl Harbor in December 1941. The President, Franklin D. Roosevelt, missed no opportunity to raise the matter when in conference with his chiefs of staff.

An air strike against the Japanese mainland seemed the most appropriate form of action, but how was this to be achieved? No bases for land planes were available within reach of the target, and the Navy's planes had a maximum range of 600 miles. To sail the carriers to within 300 miles of enemy coastline was to put them into unacceptable hazard. It seemed, within the department of Admiral Ernest J. King, Chief of Naval Operations, that the answer lay somewhere between the two. Less than a month after Pearl Harbor an idea was already taking shape that perhaps it would be possible to launch army medium bombers against Japan from aircraft carriers, a safe distance from the target. One thing was certain; it might be possible to launch medium bombers from an aircraft carrier, but there was no way that they would be able to return to it. Aeroplanes of that size were not equipped with arrester hooks, and they needed a much longer landing run than a carrier could offer.

The officers on Admiral King's staff who had dreamed up the idea were sent to discuss it with Lieutenant General H. H. Arnold, Commanding General of the Army Air Forces. General Arnold had the ideal man to evaluate the suggestion. He called in Lieutenant Colonel Jimmy Doolittle, a veteran airman with a world-wide reputation, who had won international air races, and broken world air speed records Doolittle suggested that the only medium bombers which might be able to take off, fully loaded, with a run of no more than 500 feet, were the Douglas B-23, or the the Mitchell, the

Far left: Admiral Ernest J. King, chief of naval operations, United States Navy, in January 1942. Officers on Admiral King's staff were the first to come up with a viable proposal that would satisfy the American population's lust for an attack upon the Japanese mainland to appease their anger at the onslaught on Pearl Harbor.

William F. Halsey (left), himself a qualified aviator, was appointed by Admiral Chester Nimitz, commander in chief of the Pacific Fleet, to command the Task Force that was to carry the B-25s of the Doolitle Raid to within striking distance of Tokyo. The photograph shows Halsey two years later, commanding the United States Third Fleet.

The USS *Hornet* (below left) put to sea carrying two USAAF B-25 Mitchell bombers, simply to show that it was possible for these to take off from an aircraft carrier. That being proved, the two army pilots flew back to their base with no idea why they had been asked to risk their lives in this eccentric experiment.

The B-25s of the 'Special Air Project' are tethered to the deck of USS *Hornet*, en route for the launching point. The aircraft had been fitted with new propellers, painted to prevent corrosion whilst exposed to the sea air and spray, and had extra fuel tanks in the fuselage.

North American B-25. When told that the maximum width available would be seventy-five feet, the choice was made automatically. The B-23 had a wing-span of ninety three feet, the Mitchell only sixty-seven.

Admiral King's men arranged for two B-25s to be hoisted onto the carrier USS *Hornet* at San Francisco, and they put to sea to prove that it could be done. It could. The two army pilots dragged their aircraft off the end of *Hornet's* deck, and disappeared over the horizon, back to their base, wondering what on earth they had done it for.

Meanwhile, Doolittle was arranging for modifications to be made to 24 Mitchells. Turrets were removed, leaving only the top turret with its two 0.5 inch machine guns, and one 0.3 inch gun in the nose, and extra fuel tanks were built into the space saved. The heavy radio equipment was also removed. Radio silence would be observed, and even more fuel tanks would be useful.

Early in March, volunteer crews were called together at Eglin Field, Florida, to begin training, although it would be another month before they would learn what it was that they had

The North American B-25 Mitchell was destined to take part in many famous operations during World War II, but none would eclipse the raid that Lieutenant Colonel James H. Doolittle led on Tokyo on April 18, 1942.

One of Doolittle's B-25s claws its way into the air (below left) as it leaves Shangri La, the mythical departure point in President Roosevelt's announcement to the American people of a token reprisal against Japan for the attack on Pearl Harbor.

Lieutenant Colonel Doolittle, at the controls of his Mitchell (right), aligns the aircraft with the white lines painted on the *Hornet*'s deck to ensure that his wing tip clears the carrier's island, and races his engines as he prepares to head for Tokyo.

volunteered for. They were already trained on the Mitchell, but until now they had been using a mile of runway for their take-offs. Now they were being asked to do it in one tenth of the distance. Doolittle trained with them, although he had not yet obtained permission to lead the operation. He flew to Washington to play off General Arnold against his Chief of Staff, getting each to leave the decision to the other, and returned to Eglin ready to go.

On April 1 the Mitchells flew to Alameda Air Station, Sacramento, to be loaded onto the *Hornet*, Captain Marc A. Mitscher commanding. The aircraft were lashed to the deck, and covered up, and in the middle of the morning next day they sailed, in company with two cruisers, four destroyers and a tanker. Five days later Vice-Admiral William Halsey, flying his flag in the carrier *Enterprise*, was due to leave Hawaii with a similar force, to join up and form Task Force 16 to carry out the 'Special Air Project'.

Shortly after they had passed under the Golden Gate Bridge, everyone found out, at last, what the 'special project' was to be. 'Now

hear this,' boomed Mitscher's voice over the ship's loudspeakers, 'We are bound for Tokyo.' Now the target folders were handed out, and the aircrews could begin to discuss flight plans, and bomb loads. None of them had seen a B-25 take off from a carrier, let alone tried it for themselves. And if they made it, none of them would be landing back. If not on the carrier, where? Russia? China? Russia said no. They were not at war with Japan, and were not anxious to jeopardise the fragile peace. Chiang Kai-shek, in China, had at first been supportive, but was having second thoughts, fearing reprisals from the Japs. So when Doolittle put to sea he had had no confirmation. As he was now subject to radio silence he would have to assume that by the time they took off, diplomatic channels would have everything fixed up.

Take off was planned for April 19, but early on 18th they ran into the Japanese seaborne early warning. The Japanese radar cover was not good, and to warn of impending attack they had a cordon of small look-out vessels, 650 miles from the coast. The fleet spotted Patrol

Boat Number 23, the *Nitto Maru*, and at the same time they intercepted her radio message, 'Three enemy aircraft carriers in sight.' In the murk, her look-outs had presumably mistaken one of the cruisers for a third carrier. They had not intended to take off until late afternoon the next the next day, and to make a night raid on Tokyo, but Admiral Halsey decided that, as the cat was out of the bag, the wisest move would be to get the Mitchells into the air. He gave the order to 'Launch planes', and Doolittle and his crews came dashing from their quarters below decks.

During the cruise from San Francisco the aircraft had been tested, and tested again. All that was required, while the crews received their final briefing, was to drag the covers off, load the four 500 pound bombs into each one, and top up the fuel tanks to replace any that might have leaked or evaporated. In the briefing room Doolittle reminded his men to look for targets of military significance – ports and shipping, railways and heavy industry – and to remember that the Emperor's palace was strictly off limits.

Up on deck the Mitchells were ranged in the order in which they were to take off. Because of the aircraft behind him, Doolittle had the shortest space to get into the air. To give him the best possible chance, the last in the line was balanced precariously on the end of the flight deck, its tail and half of its fuselage hanging out over the water. It would not be possible to finish loading it until they could roll it forward a little.

At 8.20 a.m., with *Hornet* charging into a 27-knot gale, Doolittle roared down the deck, keeping his nose and port wheels on the white lines painted on the deck to make sure his starboard wing tip missed the superstructure, and trying to time his run so that the pitching carrier would toss him into the air with the rise of its bows. He made it, and circled the ship to watch number two's attempt. This time the timing was not so good. The bows rose too early, and the pilot found himself struggling uphill. Staggering over the bows, he was practically brushing the crests of the waves before he gained safe flying speed, and climbed away to join his leader. Eventually they were all safely airborne. The whole operation had taken an hour, by which time

The Japanese declared that any of the Raiders who fell into their hands, either immediately after the raid or subsequently, would be punished by death. Eight of the survivors were captured, three of whom were then executed. It is unlikely that this airman, pictured in 1943, had taken part in the raid - his fate is unknown.

100

Barrack blocks at Yokosuka Naval Base (right), photographed by the copilot of crew No. 13, Lieutenant Richard Nobloch, as the crew climbed away from their attack on the base's technical buildings.

As the war progressed, and the USAAF were able to operate their heavy bombers against the Japanese mainland from captured land bases, damage was caused to enemy factories (below right), which made the Doolittle Raid more than just a token reprisal.

Doolittle was well on his way to the Japanese coast.

As soon as the last aircraft was off, Halsey spun his fleet around and headed out into the Pacific to get as much space as possible between Task Force 16 and the enemy.

The message from the *Nitto Maru* had indeed got through, and a strike force had taken off from Kisarazu, near Tokyo, to look for the fleet. They returned to base, not having found anything, although a plane on a routine patrol reported having seen a twin-engined bomber heading for Japan. This was considered extremely unlikely, and, just as at Pearl Harbor, the warning was disregarded.

Five hours after takeoff, Doolittle was bombing Tokyo. On the run in he had met many Jap aircraft, mostly training types, but some fighters. Flying as low as possible, none seemed to interfere with him, and he was not attacked except by anti-aircraft fire after he had dropped his bombs.

All of the crews reached their targets, and, with one exception, carried on into China to look for landing grounds. They had been hoping to pick up Chinese radio beacons, but none of them succeeded in doing so. The odd man out, having used more fuel than expected en route from the *Hornet*, decided that he would not make China. Instead, disregarding

The majority of Doolittle's Raiders made it safely to China, and from there back home. Another photograph from the camera of Lieutenant Nobloch, of crew No. 13, shows the rest of the crew with some of the Chinese who escorted them to safety. The incensed Japanese murdered thousands of Chinese in reprisal for the help given to the Raiders.

After thirteen hours in the air, Doolittle left his aircraft on automatic pilot and he and his crew baled out over China. The following afternoon, with all of his crew accounted for, Doolittle and his crew chief, Paul Leonard, climbed the mountainside on which their aircraft had crashed.

instructions, he headed for Russia, and found an airfield in the vicinity of Vladivostok, where the aircraft was confiscated and the crew interned.

This was the only one of the raiders to make a safe landing. Doolittle was one of eleven who, unable to find an airfield, ordered his crew to bail out. The others made forced landings, from which, in general, the crews fared less well, most being killed or injured in the process.

Doolittle and his crew had bailed out after thirteen hours in the air. They quickly regrouped on the ground, and by the morning of the 20th had got together with four other crews. Through the Embassy in Chungking, Doolittle passed a

message to General Arnold of the success of the raid.

Quickly the news was announced to the delighted American public. President Roosevelt enigmatically declared that the raid had 'taken off from Shangri-la.' The nation and the press discussed where Shangri-la really was. The idea of an aircraft carrier was suggested, but was, by and large, discounted. It was over a year before the truth was revealed, but the truth was of no great significance. What was important was that the United States of America had begun to avenge Pearl Harbor, and the nation could think about holding up its head once again.

AIR BATTLE FOR BURMA

At the end of 1943 the Japanese had resisted all attempts to deny them their hold on Burma. Now they were poised on the eastern frontier of India, threatening to pour their hordes into the sub-continent.

At this time a major conference took place in Quebec. The 'COSSAC' conference – The Chiefs of Staff to the Supreme Allied Commander – created the strategies to be adopted in all theatres of the war. One of their most imaginative decisions, aimed at blocking any further spread to the westward of Japanese domination, was the unification of all the forces in that part of the world under a single command. To be under the control of its own Supreme Allied Commander, South East Asia Command was born. Perhaps an even more imaginative decision was the choice of the man who was to be placed in command. The appointment of Admiral Lord Louis Mountbatten, a British Naval officer, was universally popular. A nephew of the King of England, he had been a dashing destroyer commander at the beginning of the war. He had become Commander in Chief of Combined Operations in the European Theatre, being responsible for such daring operations as the raids on St Nazaire and Dieppe. At the age of only 43 he was the youngest officer since Napoleon Bonaparte to be appointed Supreme Commander in the Field.

One of Mountbatten's first decisions was that all allied air operations over Burma should be integrated, and Eastern Air Command was formed. Its commander was to be Major General George E. Stratemeyer, United States Army. His new Command brought together aircrews and ground personnel from the United States, Britain, Canada, Australia, New Zealand, South Africa and India. In his first General Order,

Admiral Lord Louis Mountbatten (on the right), Supreme Allied Commander in South East Asia, talking to General Stilwell, commander of U.S. and Chinese land forces in Northern Burma. The Supreme Commander's call for total integration of the allied air operations over Burma led to the formation of Eastern Air Command, and to the great success enjoyed by the air forces under Mountbatten's command.

Air supply enabled the land forces to turn defensive situations into victories. The key to air supply was the Douglas Dakota aircraft, operated by both the American and the British crews of Eastern Air Command.

on December 15, 1943, Stratemeyer said, 'A resourceful, able and wily enemy must be blasted from the jungles of Burma, and driven from its skies. His lines of communication must be obliterated; his will to resist crushed. We must merge into one unified force,' he continued, 'in thought and deed. A force neither British nor American; a force with the virtues of each, and the faults of neither.'

Integration was what the Supreme Commander had asked for, and integration was what General Stratemeyer set about creating. The integration started at the

Headquarters, it moved forward to the bases, and on into the jungle strips. 'We'll work together', said Stratemeyer, and work together they did. American officers worked alongside British officers; British non-commissioned ranks alongside Americans. At the start the RAF contingent at the Headquarters in Queensway, New Delhi, numbered no more than 30. Twelve months later it was more than three hundred. At Headquarters the young men of many nations worked side by side, they lived and slept side by side, they ate and drank side by side. The same thing happened right down the

From their bases in Bengal, USAAF B-25 Mitchell bombers (left) crossed the 8,000-foot barrier of the mountain range which separates India from Burma to attack the enemy, often descending right down to ground level. They then had to struggle back over the barrier to return to their bases in India.

Eastern Air Command's fighter aircraft (below left) established the supremacy in the air that was necessary if the transport aircraft were to have no more than natural hazards to contend with as they supplied the land forces in the jungles and on the plains of Burma.

One of the outstanding performers of the campaign in Burma was the 'Hurri-Bomber' (right), the ground-attack version of the aircraft that had fought with such distinction during the Battle of Britain and over Malta.

line. They worked together down the line because the two men at the top worked together. General Stratemeyer and his deputy, Air Vice-Marshal T. M. 'Bill' Williams, liked each other, and got on together.

The magnitude of what they had to achieve can be seen by looking at the map of Burma and eastern India. The mountain ranges spread south into Burma from the Himalayas – Everest, and the roof of the world. For centuries they had been the barrier which had protected the west from invading forces from the east, and they served the same purpose when the Japanese set out for their 'march on Delhi'. The mountain ranges looked as though they would also be an insurmountable barrier going the other way, preventing the Allied troops in India from pushing back into Burma, and sweeping the Japanese back to where they had come from. They were a barrier 8,000 feet high, through which supplies would have to be carried to sustain an advance. There was only one road, twisting and turning through the passes – and its beginning was already 200 miles from the

docks at Calcutta, where the supplies were unloaded from their ships. At the best it was a fortnight's journey, and for the six months from May to October, during the monsoon, it would be impossible.

Eastern Air Command provided the answer. Their aircraft cut the two week journey to less than 24 hours. They carried regiment after regiment of soldiers over the mountains, and then went back, again and again, for the supplies to keep them going. Food and ammunition, fuel for the vehicles, water for the men to drink, and even mules to carry things where the vehicles could not go. 'The monsoon will put a stop to it', said the pundits, but the aircrews were not listening. They took their lives into their hands, climbed into their DC-3s and set out to do battle with the peaks, to supply the men who were doing battle with the Japanese.

The airmen won their battle with the mountains, and with the monsoons. There seemed to be nothing that they could not carry. A 155 mm howitzer was dismantled, carried over the mountains and reassembled. During July and August it helped the fighter-bombers and the B-25s to batter into submission the enemy defences at Myitkyina. The component parts of seventeen-ton bulldozers were lifted over, put back together, and used to carve airstrips out of the jungle.

The combat aircraft had the same mountain barrier to contend with each time they went into action. USAAF B-25s and RAF Beaufighters, airborne from their bases in Bengal, would climb to 16,000 feet to cross the rocky peaks; peaks which, more often than not, were pushing up into a thick layer of cloud. Once over, they would swoop down almost to ground level, to attack the Rangoon to Mandalay railway. Often they would suffer battle damage from the railway's anti-aircraft defences. Then, perhaps with an engine missing, or losing fuel, they would turn for home, faced with the struggle back over the mountains, on their 500 mile journey back to their base, and safety. Many made it, but many did not. They simply vanished. The thick, green, jungle-clad mountain sides became their war graves.

Time and time again, the supply aircraft of the Command helped the men on the ground to resist Japanese counterattacks. The soldiers, besieged in defensive circles, were sustained by air supply. From first light until dusk, hundreds of tons of supplies cascaded in, beneath their parachute canopies. Rations, fuel, ammunition, drinking water and medical supplies rained down to the encircled troops. The Japanese surrounding them had no such succour. Eastern Air Command's fighter aircraft – P.47 and P.38, Hurricane and Spitfire – had established their supremacy in the air. It was the besiegers, not the besieged, who starved and suffered from thirst. The Japanese wavered, broke, and faded away.

In March of 1944, the 14th Army, in northern Burma, was hit by three of Japan's finest fighting divisions, at Imphal and Kohima. It was vital that they should not be allowed to break through. If they had done so they would have been able to slip around the end of the mountain range, and into India. Again, Eastern Air Command's aircraft came to the rescue. The whole of the 5th (Indian) and the 7th

The ground crew of a P.38 fighter attend to the long-range fuel tanks of their aircraft. These tanks were vital if the fighters were to have any useful endurance for combat after their passage over the mountains from India.

A Mitsubishi Ki-21 'Sally' on the ground is attacked by parachute fragmentation bombs. These bombs, dropped from a low level, were a potential danger to the aircraft delivering them. The use of parachutes to delay the bombs' fall ensured that the attacking aircraft had passed to a safe distance before the explosion.

Left: ground crewmen loading rocket projectiles onto the underwing pylons of a Royal Air Force ground-attack Beaufighter.

The Republic P.47 Thunderbolt was another American-built aircraft that saw service in Burma. Below: an RAF ground crew watches as a 'vic' of three Thunderbolts makes a classic low-level pass over the airfield.

(Indian) Divisions were flown in to assist, lock, stock and barrel. The Japanese were held, but their advance had cut the supply lines. Once again everything had to be brought in by air. Here, with the open spaces of the Imphal Plain, the aircraft could land to unload. As much as 400 tons of supplies were flown in every day. And the aircraft did not return empty. Noncombatant personnel, who had been very useful when Imphal had been not much more than a garrison area, were now an unacceptable drain on the resources which had to be flown in. So the returning aircraft evacuated them, along with the casualties. Some of the casualties had been brought out of clearings in the jungle, onto the plain, by light aircraft operating in the most hazardous

circumstances. In May alone, over 30,000 noncombatants and casualties were airlifted out.

In the face of air supply to the defenders, and air attack upon their own lines, the Japanese faltered, stopped, then began to fall back. It was the beginning of the end of the Japanese occupation of Burma. Even the monsoon did not protect them – a monsoon during which 175 inches of rain fell on northern Burma. In four months of the worst flying weather in the world, over the worst flying territory in the world, the fighter-bombers and the light bombers of the 3rd Tactical Air Force flew over 24,000 sorties. By the end of August the last of the attackers had been thrown back into Burma. The long retreat had started. It continued

TURNTABLE

ENGINE SHEDS

COAL STACKS

SIDINGS WITH TRUCKS

The Japanese supply system was a routine target for Eastern Air Command's aircraft. Left: an annotated reconnaissance photograph shows the results of an RAF attack on the railway yards at Mandalay.

Shipping also came in for its share of Eastern Air Command's offensive against the Japanese transport system. Below left: an RAF aircraft dives to attack coastal shipping in the small harbour at Akyab.

Phosphorus incendiary bombs were another way of destroying enemy aircraft caught on the ground on their airfields.

for 1,000 miles; back to Mandalay, and then on to Rangoon.

By May 1945 the task had been accomplished. Rangoon, the capital of Burma, had been retaken. The road to China was open. Oil was flowing 2,000 miles from Calcutta to the United States airmen who were operating in China. Eastern Air Command's aircraft, with machine gun, rocket and bomb, had rooted the Japanese air force out of its airfields, and, as General Stratemeyer had demanded at the beginning, had driven them from the skies of Burma. They had achieved more than Mountbatten had asked for. A 1,000 mile way had been blasted through the jungle for the

14th Army, from Imphal to Rangoon. Supply aircraft had kept the army moving through jungle and swamp, across the dust bowl of the plains, and over mountain ranges. They had smashed bridges and supply lines, and burned stock piles into blackened ruins. They had left ships sinking in the harbours, and sampans riddled with bullets on the rivers. They had torn up the enemy's railway tracks, set fire to his trains, and wiped out his road transport.

The men on the ground, British and American, Pathan, Sikh and Rajput, Chinese and African, all had good reason to turn their eyes to the sky, and say, in their various tongues, 'Thank God for the Air Force.'

ENTER THE MIGHTY 8TH

At the time that hostilities began between America and Japan, and the United States declared war on Germany, General H.H. Arnold was Commanding General of the United States Army Air Forces. He declared that the number one job of the Air Force should be bombardment. 'We must have long-range bombers which can hit the enemy before he hits us.' he said. 'In short, the best defence is attack.' He expressed the commitment of the Air Force to daylight bombing, with precision bombsights. Their object was to be 'strategic precision bombing deep in the enemy's territory, of key targets such as airplane factories, aluminium plants, and submarine building bases.

'To pursue these objects from the American homeland was obviously an impossibility, and so, less than eight weeks after the declarations of war, the General signed an order which was to lead to the establishment of an American air force in Britain. Less than a month later the nucleus of the headquarters of the USAAF 8th Air Force Bomber Command, lead by Brigadier

The B-17C had been used by the Royal Air Force in Europe since 1940. Many of its faults were corrected in the B-17E, the first Flying Fortress that the 8th Air Force took to England, and used for their first operation, a raid against the railway marshalling yard at Rouen, France, on August 15, 1942.

114

The first bombing raid in Europe that the 8th Air Force took part in was made in American-built aircraft with RAF markings. The aircraft were Douglas Bostons (above) and the raid, against Luftwaffe airfields in Holland, took place on July 4, 1942.

General Ira C. Eaker, arrived on British soil. General Arnold's order instructed Eaker to 'make the necessary preparation to insure competent and aggressive command and direction of our bomber units in England.'

Brigadier Eaker and his companions had no time to play the tourist when they arrived in London, but they were not blind, and their first sight of the British capital made quite an impression on them. After a year and a half of air attack, they could not fail to notice London's bomb damage. Aerial bombardment was what they were here to organize, and, all around them, was a clear illustration of its destructive capabilities. They could not miss the impact of one of the side effects of aerial bombardment. They could not avoid the restrictions imposed

by the strict blackout which was observed in Britain for protection against enemy bombers after dark, nor could they avoid the restrictions of the food rationing suffered by the inhabitants of a blockaded island.

They were faced by a big job, but their hosts, the RAF, had over two years experience, and they were quite prepared to share it. The RAF had not had a good experience of daylight bombing, and never really lost their scepticism of the policy of daylight raids. Flying their obsolescent Fairey Battle and Bristol Blenheim bombers during the early months of their war with Germany, the RAF had suffered ferocious attrition losses, and had been driven to practise their craft during the hours of darkness. It would not be until after the Allies had established a

Left: ground crewmen of the 8th Air Force prepare a B-17 for operations. In the early days in Europe, the B-17s were delivered with an olive-drab finish to the sides and upper surfaces, and with gray undersides.

One of the last tasks to be carried out before the B-17s departed on operations was loading the bombs. The composition of the bomb load has been decided, and (right) the armourers winch the bombs from their trolleys into the bomb bay.

foothold back in 'Fortress Europe', in late 1944, that they would again venture out in significant numbers in daylight. However, if the USAAF thought they could do it, the RAF were prepared to give whatever help they could. And having the 'Yanks' operating during the day could have a good knock-on effect. The German defenders would not be able to spend the daylight hours resting up, as they did now, ready for the 'Limey's' raid the next night.

Cooperation between the two air forces began straight away. RAF airfields had to be taken over, and any necessary alterations put in hand. American intelligence men arrived in advance of the combat crews, and helped to debrief the RAF aircrews returning from their operations. In this way valuable experience of the conduct of bombing operations was acquired, and passed back to help with the 8th Air Force's planning and training.

Appropriately, the first time that American aircrew, flying American-built aircraft, ventured forth against the enemy was 4th July. Admittedly the aircraft were not wearing USAAF markings;

they were Douglas Bostons (A.20s) belonging to a RAF squadron. To shepherd the Americans through this historic first operation, half of the twelve aircraft taking part were crewed by the RAF. The targets were enemy airfields in Holland. Unfortunately, some way out from the enemy coast they flew over a 'spotter' ship, placed there specifically to give early warning of incoming air raids, and the German gunners were standing by when the aircraft arrived over the target. The first 'V' of three, lead by a RAF-flown aircraft, with USAAF crew on each wing, approached their target through an intense barrage. The pilot of the RAF crew said it was the worst he had ever experienced - one of the Americans said the same thing. The Americans had been warned not to fly straight and level, or to perform elegant, smooth curves, but they did not realise just how erratically they needed to fly for safety at low altitude. One was hit and crashed in flames. The other was badly damaged in the nose and one wing. An engine burst into flames, and, as the 'plane staggered, the belly struck the ground. The pilot hauled it

117

back into the air on one engine. He thought about a forced landing, changed his mind, and managed to get the Boston back to base. When his report finished up on Eaker's desk, the General wrote across it, 'This officer is hereby awarded the Distinguished Service Cross.' Of the others who got back to base, three were given the Distinguished Flying Cross. But the mission had not been an unqualified success. Two crews brought back their bombs, having failed to identify the target as they swept across fast at low level. The other two bombed their target alright, but one of them was shot down. It could have been better, but the ice had been broken. The 8th had gone to war.

They now began to prepare for the real business. The same day as the Boston raid, the first of the 8th Air Force's B-17Es arrived in Britain. By August two Groups had been formed, and the task of training for the daylight operations began in earnest. In 1940 the British aircraft had not been equipped for the task, nor had they developed suitable techniques to minimise the losses. The training of the American crews had already been aimed at flying daylight missions, and although the RAF tried to encourage the USAAF to join them in the dark, they would have needed to retrain completely. This would have significantly delayed them achieving full operational status. The RAF had flown loose formations, with a few comparatively lightweight machine guns in each aircraft. The 8th. were going to fly as many aircraft as possible, in tight formations. Each aircraft would carry ten 0.5 in. machine guns, and so long as the formation retained its integrity the aircraft would afford each other mutual protection. Eaker drove his crews to train hard to fly tighter and tighter formations. They also had to learn to contend with the uncertainties of the European weather, and with the congestion of the airspace over a small island which was becoming so crowded with airfields that it was quite common for crews to miss their own field altogether, and land at the one next door.

The first trial of strength was planned for August 10. The commander of RAF Bomber

The B-17 Flying Fortress was in great demand when America entered the war. Immediately after Pearl Harbor the delivery schedule of the Boeing production plant at Seattle was accelerated. This was, perhaps, the workers' response to the atrocity at Honolulu, and during the first month even the accelerated schedule was exceeded by seventy percent.

General Henry H. Arnold, commander of the U.S. Army Air Forces, was the first army airman to achieve the rank of full general, after long and distinguished service. As commanding general, he declared that 'the best defence is attack', and expressed the commitment of the USAAF to precision daylight bombing deep within the enemy's territory.

Just twelve aircraft took part in the 8th's first operation, against Rouen. Soon the formations consisted of hundreds of aircraft - massive formations which took an hour or more to assemble, as they wheeled above the English countyside (left) before turning east and setting course for the target.

The long daylight transits over enemy territory inevitably resulted in many aircraft sustaining damage, from either anti-aircraft gunfire or intercepting fighters. Damage to the fuel system could mean the loss of vital range, and result in failure to reach base. If the hydraulics were damaged, the probable outcome was a belly landing (below left) with the wheels still retracted.

Command, Air Marshal Sir Arthur Harris, was not pleased to learn that Eaker planned to take part in it himself. Harris' argument was that during the last six months the RAF had put a lot of effort into teaching Eaker all they had learned since 1939, much of it highly classified. With their lack of confidence in daylight operations, Harris and his staff had visions of having to start the induction over again with Eaker's successor, and, even worse, of having someone with their highest level of intelligence information falling into enemy hands. (On the few occasions that RAF star-rank officers flew on operations, they did so under an assumed name, wearing the uniform of a much lower rank, to reduce the risk of deep interrogation if they were shot down and captured.) Eaker's response was that he would find it difficult to send his men into danger which he had not experienced himself. Harris himself had flown operations in World War I.

Predictably, the weather intervened. The raid was rescheduled – again the weather did not play ball. Telegrams were received from General Arnold in Washington. 'Why are the 8th's aircraft still on the ground?' In the squadrons morale was wearing thin from repeated 'dry runs', bad weather and a general impatience to get at the Hun.

Eventually the weather let up. At 1526 on August 17 the first Fortress took off. In rapid succession it was followed by eleven more. They flew in two sections of six. Eaker flew in the lead ship of the second section. He had had himself put through a gunnery course, to comply with his own standing order that no passengers were to be carried on operational flights. Anyone who went along had to be able to pull his weight. He took his place in the radio operator's top turret, but there is no record that he had to fire his guns in anger. Crossing the sea to the enemy coast there was no danger of him having to do so. They had made a good rendezvous with RAF Spitfires, which escorted them until they reached the limit of their range, from where the B-17s only had thirty-five miles or so to go to their target, the railway marshalling yards at Rouen.

For over three hours those left behind – ground crew as well as spare aircrew –waited anxiously. Then, just before 1900 hours, a gaggle of specks appeared. As they got closer the

watchers counted. Nine, ten, eleven – at last they could make out number twelve. The 8th. Air Force Bomber Command, USAAF, had flown its first daylight bombardment mission, and everyone had come home.

As the months and the years passed, the missions carried on. The formations got bigger, the routes got longer - much longer. The loss rate did not stay at zero. Between August 1939 and September 1945, RAF Bomber Command lost over 47,000 aircrew killed. In a war which lasted two years less, the 'Mighty 8th', as it became known, lost 26,000 in combat, almost one in eleven of all the American airmen who crossed the Atlantic to fight for freedom from the airfields of Britain.

Corporate identity in World War II. The crew have named their aircraft 'Cabin in the Sky', and this is repeated on the back of their flying jackets.

As the strength of the 8th Air Force built up, their massed formations returned day after day to attack 'Fortress Europe'. Their sophisticated bombsights, used in daylight, enabled them to strike their targets accurately from high altitude, resulting in concentrated devastation. Their equipment and training were both geared to daylight operations, and were the reason that the USAAF did not join the RAF in the latter's attacks on the enemy under cover of darkness.

THE DAMBUSTERS

Science and technology has never played such a major part in warfare as during World War II. And no scientist or technologist had achieved such spectacular and eccentric results as Doctor Barnes Wallis, an engineer working for the Vickers Aircraft Company in Britain. Not that the projects for which he will be remembered in the history books were carried out in the course of his work for Vickers. They were projects that he dreamed up in his spare time, although the Vickers connection had its uses. 'Why on earth should we lend you a Wellinaton bomber?', said a harassed official at Bomber Command Headquarters, when Wallis wanted to test the prototype of one of his schemes. 'Well, I did design it!', retorted Wallis.

In addition to its aircraft interests, Vickers was engaged in a wide variety of heavy engineering such as steel works, and ship building. Wallis was, therefore, well aware of the huge quantities of water required by industries of this nature. Germany's heavy industry was concentrated in the Ruhr, and the vast quantities of water came from the lakes formed by four or five dams. Wallis conjectured that if some, or all, of these dams could be

For normal operations, the gigantic bomb bay of the Lancaster could accommodate both a huge 4,000 pounder and a collection of 500-pound incendiaries. This particular aircraft, 'S' for Sugar of 467 Squadron, is now on display in the Royal Air Force Museum at Hendon, London.

The Avro Lancaster seemed the obvious aircraft to select to carry the amazing weapon devised by Doctor Barnes Wallis for the attack on the Ruhr dams. The photograph shows Lancasters being assembled at a plant 'somewhere in England' - the euphemism that was used throughout the war to refer to any location.

destroyed, then for a time at least the German war effort would be disrupted. The problem was to work out how it could be done.

Conventional bombing was not going to be the answer. The dams, by their very nature, were designed to withstand great stress. A direct hit would just bounce off. The blast of a near miss on the 'dry' side would be deflected harmlessly into space by the massive structure of the dam, whilst the effect of a near miss which fell into the lake would simply be absorbed by the water. Or would it? Wallis had a theory that if the bomb were to explode flush against the wall of the dam, and close to the base, the incompressibility of millions of gallons

of water in the lake would direct the whole effect of the bomb-burst into the wall itself. It was doubtful whether a single bomb, even one precisely placed, would be sufficient. But if a whole series of bombs could be delivered accurately, the battering ram effect of the explosions, all in the same place, would eventually cause the dam to give way.

The answer might be a torpedo. But torpedoes of sufficient size did not exist, and, in any case, the Germans had already thought of that one. The dams were protected by anti-torpedo nets strung across the lakes.

Wallis's eventual solution was quite simple in its scientific principle, but seemed impossible

in practice. His idea was based on the childhood game of 'ducks and drakes'. A specially designed bomb would be released from low level so that it would skip along the surface of the lake, hopping over the protective torpedo nets, until it hit the dam wall. It would then sink down the face of the wall, when a delayed action fuse would detonate it in the required place.

After many weeks of experiment Wallis had produced a weapon which he believed would do the job, and he had been allowed to use one of 'his' Wellingtons to test a prototype. In fact, a series of prototypes had to be tested, because the impact with the water was so severe that the first ones disintegrated. The greater the height from which the weapon was dropped, the stronger, and therefore the heavier, it had to be. He found that, if the weight was to be kept within reasonable limits,

it had to be dropped from no higher than 60 feet.

The weapon, code named 'Upkeep', looked like a giant oil drum. To ensure that it detonated at the correct depth a hydrostatic fuse was fitted, instead of a delayed action one. In essence, it was an overgrown depth charge. Officially it was listed as a mine. The only problem now was how to deliver it.

Despite the increase in weight when it was strengthened to withstand the impact, it could still be carried by a Lancaster. (It weighed 9,250lbs, including 6,600lbs of explosive.) But carrying it was the least of the problems. As well as the need for his weapon to be dropped from precisely 60 feet above the surface of the water, Wallis required the aircraft to be travelling at exactly 220 mph. The wings had to be level at the moment of release, or the weapon would strike the water edge first, and would

The Lancasters on the Dams Raid flew in close formation, but at tree-top height. The pilots had to remain on manual control throughout the flight, to avoid buildings, trees and electricity pylons. Maintaining strict radio silence, the wireless operators conducted conversations between the aircraft by using signalling lamps.

Twenty Lancasters were modified to carry Wallis's 'Upkeep' weapon, and were listed as B.1 (Special). The serial number of these aircraft had a suffix 'G', which meant 'Guard', and indicated that they should be kept under strict security. For this reason there are few photographs of 617 Squadron's B.1 (Special) Lancasters.

veer off course. But perhaps most difficult of all, it had to be dropped not more than 450 yards, and not less than 400 yards, from the dam wall. At 220 mph the Lancaster would pass through the dropping zone in half a second.

All the time that Wallis had been perfecting his scheme (in his own time and at his own expense) he had been trying to convince the authorities that they should put it into action. It was early in 1943. If the attack was to take place that year, it should really happen around the end of May. At that time the lakes would be at their fullest following the spring thaw. Once May was past the water level would begin to drop, and would carry on dropping until the next year. At the end of February the go ahead was given. There were, at the most, twelve weeks left in which to find the men who could do the job, train them, and put the plan into effect.

Obviously, to achieve Wallis's parameters for delivering 'Upkeep', the training was going to be lengthy. Air Marshal Sir Arthur Harris,

Commander-in-Chief of Bomber Command, did not want to take an active squadron out of service for the time that would be necessary – the Command was already pretty busy. One way to reduce the training time would be to use only experienced crews. Harris decided to form a new squadron of hand picked aircrew, and he knew who he wanted as its leader.

On the night of 15 March 1943, Wing Commander Guy Gibson, 24 years old, flew his 173rd operation of the war, to complete his third 'tour'. He was due for a break – he had not had one since the war began three and a half years earlier. On Harris' instructions, Gibson was invited to do 'just one more trip' before taking his break. Because the operation, to be code named 'Chastise', was Top Secret, he had to make his decision with no more information than that 'it is important'. He accepted.

Within a week Gibson's crews were beginning to arrive, and 617 Squadron came into being. Everyone had completed at least two tours, or were on the verge of doing so. This

To conserve fuel for the long journey, the pilots used only the inboard engines while taxying (left) and waiting their turn to take off.

Parallel rulers and a cup of coffee (right) are two essential accessories in the Flight Planning room, as the crews study their maps, to select a route which will enable them to penetrate to the heart of Germany at low level, without crossing any major flak concentrations.

Below right: in a photograph taken five months before the Dams Raid, Wing Commander Guy Gibson poses for the camera with his pipe and the aircrew from his previous squadron.

was the cream of Bomber Command.

Training began in earnest, although even Gibson still did not know what they were training for. Within the training they had to devise ways of meeting the requirements for dropping 'Upkeep', again without knowing why they were doing it. The height was achieved by fitting spot-lights under the aircraft. One under the nose angled aft, and one under the tail angled forwards. When at the correct height, the lights on the water would align side by side, to form a figure eight. To gauge the range, the bomb aimer had a wooden isosceles triangle, with a peep-hole at the apex, and a pin at either end of the base. Spying through the hole, he waited until the pins became superimposed upon the towers on the dam,

and then pressed the bomb release. The flight engineer sat beside the pilot, calling out the speed, to maintain a constant 220 mph.

To reduce the risk of detection by radar, the trip was to be flown the whole way at low level, and either the approach or the overshoot at each dam was through a tortuous mountain valley. So the mission would need a clear sky with a fairly full moon.

Everything seemed right on 16 May, and Operation 'Chastise' took off.

Gibson led the first wave of nine aircraft, with the Möhne Dam its primary target, and the Eder as the secondary. A second wave, consisting of five aircraft, was heading for the dam at Sorpe, while a third wave, also of five aircraft, was to act as an airborne reserve,

Below: the 'bouncing bomb' in the modified bomb bay of a 617 Squadron aircraft. '"G" for George' was the personal aircraft of the squadron's commander, Wing Commander Guy Gibson.

Right: a reconnaissance shot, taken the day after the attack, of the gap in the Möhne Dam and the low water level in the reservoir.

supporting either of the other two waves as required. If not needed they were to attack minor dams independently.

After making the first run over the target himself, Gibson remained over the lake, flying in with each of the following aircraft in turn, advising the pilot over the radio, and distracting the aim of the anti-aircraft defenses. After six aircraft had bombed, the dam collapsed, and a vast torrent of water rushed down the valley. Gibson then led the remaining three Lancasters to the Eder, which was also destroyed. Meanwhile, only one aircraft of the second wave had succeeded in reaching the Sorpe, and managed to inflict only minor damage. Two of the reserve aircraft were ordered to follow up, but by the time they arrived the valley was filling with mist, which hampered their attack. The other two reserve aircraft were sent to separate alternative targets, but one was not successful, and the other was shot down before it arrived.

Eight of the nineteen aircraft which took part in Operation 'Chastise' failed to return, with the loss of 56 men. On their return to base

the crews were so exhausted that they parked their aircraft in the first available dispersal. As a result, it was several days before many of the ground crews discovered whether or not the aircraft which they had dispatched had survived.

Considerable damage was caused by the raid, but without having the devastating effect which had been hoped. However, there was a considerable 'knock-on' effect. The anti-aircraft defences at the dams were immediately strengthened, the guns being committed for the rest of the war, although the dams were never attacked again. Repairs to the dams were not completed until the end of August, and to achieve this many hundreds of construction workers had to be withdrawn from work on the defences on the Channel coast in preparation for the invasion.

For his part in the raid Gibson was awarded the Victoria Cross. He turned down promotion to Group Captain (full Colonel), which would have taken him away from operational flying. He was shot down in a Mosquito during his fourth tour, and is buried in Holland.

With smiles of relief on their faces, and loaded with equipment, a crew make their way to the transport that will take them to interrogation.

ATTACK ON SCHWEINFURT

P.47 Thunderbolt escort fighters of the 8th Air Force Fighter Command, together with the P.38 Lightnings, could escort the bombers across occupied Europe as far as the German border. Until the long-range P.51 Mustangs came along later in the war, the bombers could carry on into Germany if they wished, but they had to take care of themselves.

By the middle of 1943 Ira C. Eaker had been been promoted to Major General, and assumed command of the whole of the 8th Air Force from Major General Carl A. Spaatz. The 8th's Bomber Command, infinitely bigger than it had been at the time of the Rouen raid just twelve months before, was now commanded by Brigadier General Frederick L. Anderson. The Air Force also had a Fighter Command now. Equipped with the Lockheed P.38 (Lightning), and the P.47 (Thunderbolt), Fighter Command could escort the B-17s to targets throughout France and Belgium. But Eaker and Anderson had plans to send the Fortresses further still. There were some juicy targets deep inside Germany, but to attack these the bombers would have to soldier on alone from the German border. The pick of these targets was Schweinfurt. A small town of some 60,000 inhabitants, in Bavaria, it occupied a

disproportionately large place in Germany's industrial war effort. Ball bearings were vital in the production of vehicles, ships and aeroplanes, and half of Germany's ball bearings were produced in five factories clustered together in Schweinfurt.

To celebrate the first anniversary of their raid on Rouen, Eaker and Anderson were planning something which would be an air battle rather than an air raid; an operation which would be of far-reaching strategic importance. The main target would be Schweinfurt. An attack on a secondary target, to be carried out a little earlier, would distract the German defences from the attack on Schweinfurt. The decoy mission would involve even deeper penetration into German territory. It was to fly right across Germany, practically to the Czechoslovakian border, to attack the Messerschmitt factory complex at Regensburg. The B-17s attacking

133

this target would not have enough fuel to return to England, and would fly straight on to American bases in North Africa. Maybe this would confuse the German fighters. Perhaps they would be sitting on the ground waiting for the Regensburg attackers to return, while the second phase was attacking Schweinfurt. General Eaker said, 'This battlefield is going to be a thousand miles long, and five miles up in the air. It will be fought in sub-zero temperatures, and the gladiators will wear oxygen masks.'

The plan of action was that 147 B-17s of the Fourth Bombardment Wing would cross the North Sea at eight o'clock in the morning, to attack the Messerschmitt works, over three hours flying away. Ten minutes later a further 230 bombers of the First Bombardment Wing would take off, hoping to slip through the German defences to Schweinfurt. The aircraft heading for Regensburg were expected to take the brunt of the attacks of the German fighters, so they would have the benefit of the escorts. The escorts would then return to refuel and rearm, and by the time the Schweinfurt aircraft had fought their way back from the target to the German border, they would be out again to meet them and bring them home.

The Regensburg force got airborne pretty well on time, and collected their fighter escort, augmented by several squadrons of RAF

Nicknamed 'Knockout Dropper', a Flying Fortress lines up on the runway whilst the ground crew line up on the grass beside her, waving their good wishes as she sets out on yet another mission. 'Knockout Dropper' was one of the aircraft that went to Schweinfurt – and came safely home.

The nose of this B-17G Flying Fortress tells the story of a hectic operational life. Each bomb painted on the nose represents a journey over enemy territory, but none of its operations can have been as desperate as the trip to Schweinfurt on August 17, 1943.

Spitfires. Almost as soon as they entered enemy airspace, over Holland and then Belgium, the first of the flak began to come up to meet them, and then the German fighters. From then on, until they reached Regensburg, almost two hours later, the battle was continuous. The Germans had learned that it was unprofitable to put all their eggs in one basket. There had been a time when they would have sent up all their fighters in a mass, at the outset, but they had realised that any bombers which escaped this onslaught then had a relatively unopposed journey to their targets. Their technique now was to spread out the fighters along the most likely route to be taken by the bomber stream, so that it could be subjected to continuous attacks. They had also established 'turn round'

airfields, so that the fighters could land where they ran out of ammunition, and wait to have a second go at the bombers as they were on their way home.

To begin with the fighters sniped cautiously at the fringes of the bomber formations, not wishing to get themselves too involved with the fighter escorts. Their turn would come at about Aachen, when the P.47s and P.38s turned for home. Meanwhile the flak gunners could help themselves.

It was relatively uncommon for a B-17 to be shot down by flak, although spectacular direct hits were seen. With the shells fused to explode at the height at which the bombers were flying, the formations were jostled by explosions, and showered with jagged, red-hot lumps of

This patch of sky represents no more than a single tile in the whole mosaic of the massed formation of the 8th Air Force which left eastern England to attack Schweinfurt, as they had done to attack so many other targets in occupied Europe.

Right: flying so high that the sky above them seems almost black, the Fortresses are picked out by the sun, and twinkle like fireflies. Their escorts climb even higher, and begin to mark the sky above the formation with vapour trails.

The Germans protected their coastline against raiding aircraft with 'flak ships'. Inland, besides the siting of permanent flak batteries, they had mobile batteries on railway trucks. Below right: gunners run to man their weapons as an air-raid warning sounds.

Left: the formations of Flying Fortresses fly high above the cloud tops, the exhaust from their engines leaving vapour trails behind them. The bright sunlight at high level and the telltale trails made the camouflage paint jobs of the Fortresses pointless. Around the time of the Schweinfurt raid, camouflage was abandoned, and replacement aircraft were delivered with a natural metal finish.

Right: on the edge of the stratosphere the Fortresses run in to their target, their bomb doors open. Flak probes the sky around them, and punctuates the formation with the black puffs of exploding shells.

shrapnel. The shrapnel caused injuries, and often deaths, among the bomber crews, and damaged their aircraft. If the damage was sufficient to cause them to drop out of the formation they would fall prey to the fighters, who could tear them to shreds at their leisure.

Aachen passed beneath them, and as it did so the escort fighters saluted and turned for home. The bombers huddled tighter together. The German attackers became more aggressive. They had learned that the weakest point of defence of the B-17s was dead ahead. To the side and rear they could direct the fire of six, and sometimes eight, of their 0.5 in. machine guns at their attackers. Directly ahead they could defend themselves with only two guns, or at best four. Throughout the fifteen mile length of the stream of bombers, the German single engined and twin engined fighters dived head on at the formations. B-17s cartwheeled out of line, and spun down towards the earth. Sometimes parachutes blossomed behind them as they fell. Ten meant that the whole crew had escaped. Often it was less; sometimes

none at all. The remaining aircraft moved forward to fill the gaps, and keep the formation tight. One squadron commander commented, 'Our navigator has an easy job today. All he has to do is follow the burning Fortresses and the parachutes of the Group up ahead of us.'

Two and a half hours after after leaving the shores of England, the Fortresses began their run in to Regensburg. The leader, Colonel Curtis E. LeMay, was surprised that at this time the fighters seemed to leave them alone, and the anti-aircraft fire fell quiet. Over the next twenty-five minutes the formation dropped over 300 tons of bombs onto the Messerschmitt works at Regensburg. The Norden bombsight, said to be capable of putting a bomb into a barrel from 30,000 feet, did its work well. By the time the formation passed on its way, not a building remained undamaged.

As they made their way towards North Africa the fighters returned, and stayed with them until they reached the Alps. From then on their only enemy was lack of fuel, and the effects of damage that they had received getting this

A B-17 flies over its target (left), the work of its colleagues already apparent on the ground below.

One of the most frightening aspects of the daylight bombing war was the sight of comrades being anihilated. The aircraft were struck more often by shrapnel fragments from bursting shells, than by direct hits from the shells themselves. Right: when an aircraft was caught by a direct hit the result was both spectacular and horrifying.

far. When they were eventually on the ground they found that they had lost 24 of their aircraft – one aircraft out of every six that had taken off. But that was not the end of it. The facilities in North Africa were inadequate to make 55 of the badly damaged Fortresses sufficiently airworthy for the return flight to Britain.

Meanwhile, back on the airfields in Britain, the 230 bombers that should have followed LeMay's formations into Germany had been prevented from taking off by bad weather over their bases. It was not until almost midday that they eventually began to get into the air. It then took one and a half hours to assemble the formations before setting course for their target. Just as, in 1940, the RAF's radar operators had watched the Luftwaffe massing over France for their attacks on southern England, the Germans were aware of what was happening, and were ready for them even before they headed for Holland.

Because of the delay, any benefit which might have been obtained from the decoy attack on Regensburg had disappeared. If anything, it had only served to alert the German defenders. Despite the fighter escort which they had across Holland and Belgium, the German fighters weighed in with enthusiasm. As well as their machine guns and 20mm cannon, some of them carried 210mm rockets which they launched into the formations from half a mile or more away. One of the Fortresses received a direct hit, and was literally blown in half, crashing to earth in flames with the whole crew trapped on board. Other fighters trailed electrically detonated bombs, capable of severing a bomber's wing, from cables beneath their aircraft.

During the journey to Schweinfurt the First Bombardment Group lost 21 aircraft. Another was caught by flak over the target. On the return trip fourteen more were lost before the

The sky is filled from horizon to horizon with Flying Fortresses and bursting flak shells. This photograph was taken during the second attack on Schweinfurt on October 14, 1943.

'Bombs away' - the bombardiers work is done. The 'Norden' bombsight can be switched off, and control of the B-17 returns to the pilot for the journey back to England.

escort fighters returned to cover their withdrawal. The loss rate of one in six, suffered by the Regensburg attack, was repeated, and by the time aircraft damaged beyond repair were taken into account, the aggregate loss rate of the two operations amounted to one in three of the aircraft taking part.

The targets at Schweinfurt were more dispersed than at Regensburg, so much so that as the smoke from the bombs of the leading aircraft drifted across the targets, it

made aiming difficult, and the accuracy and effect of the bombing suffered. Ball bearing production was restored a little over a week after the attack, although production was reduced by thirty-five percent. It was not good enough.

Bombardment crews of the 8th Air Force attended a briefing on October 14. A hush fell upon the room when the cover was drawn back from the briefing-board to reveal the target. They were going back to Schweinfurt.

PLOESTI-THE VITAL MISSION

One third of Germany's oil supplies came from the Rumanian oilfields and refineries at Ploesti. Here was a prime strategic target for aerial bombardment, but one which seemed to be out of reach of the Allied air forces. Frequently during the latter part of 1942 and early 1943, Winston Churchill proposed an alliance with Turkey as a means of obtaining air bases from which attacks on Ploesti could be launched.

After the Anglo-US Casablanca Conference of February 1943, plans were made to attack the Rumanian oil industry by a long-range mission of B-24 (Liberator) bombers from the US Ninth Air Force in North Africa. The task of the detailed planning for the operation, to be codenamed 'Tidal Wave', was given to Colonel Jacob Smart, of General Arnold's USAAF Headquarters in America. Smart flew to North Africa by way of England, where he collected intelligence on the Ploesti refineries from the RAF.

The round trip for the B-24s was going to be well over 2,000 miles, mostly over enemy territory, and without any benefit of fighter escort. Smart produced a startling plan for the mission in an attempt to minimise these disadvantages: it would be carried out at low level. This proposal surprised all who heard it. Not only was it unconventional, but the B-24 was notoriously unsuited to low-level operations. Smart demolished objections with reasoned arguments. The sheer audacity of a low-level approach would give the element of surprise, and the Liberators would remain undetected by enemy radar for the longest possible time. It would reduce the time during which individual flak units could engage the attackers, and it would limit the defending fighters to interceptions from above only. Perhaps most important, it would aid target identification and attack accuracy. Not more than 200 aircraft would be available for the attack. Only

Left: a typical B-24 Liberator crew. Four officers and five enlisted men, brought together from the four corners of the United States, line up for a photograph in front of the aircraft in which they will go into battle.

Now in its own element, a Liberator (right) is airborne and heading for its target.

The armourers 'give dreadful note of preparation', as William Shakespeare put it. The fuses have been fitted to the bombs, and their trolleys wheeled beneath the bulky, low-slung fuselage of a B-24. For the Ploesti raid delayed-action fuses were used so that the low-flying Liberators were not blown up by the explosion of their own bombs.

the seven most vital refineries would be targeted, and even then the attack would have to be directed at specific installations within these refineries. Such accuracy could only be accomplished from low level. The difficulty of low flying in the B-24 would be overcome by training. .

The units allocated to 'Tidal Wave' were 98th and 376th Bombardment Groups, already serving with the Ninth Air Force, the newly formed and inexperienced 389th Bombardment Group, and 44th and 93rd Bombardment Groups, attached to the Ninth Air Force from General Eaker's Eighth Air Force in Britain. From July 20, 1943 all five units were withdrawn from other operations to concentrate on intensive low flying formation practice at Benghazi in Libya. The object of the training had not been revealed to the crews.

Royal Air Force photo-interpretation technicians in England built a 1:5,000 three-dimensional scale model of the Ploesti oil fields and refineries, which they completed within a week. This was flown out to North Africa, and their target was announced to the five Groups training in Libya. A quite new departure was the production of a documentary film about the target, to assist with crew briefings. The calm, reassuring voice of the Air Force public relations expert explained to the crews that the defences which would confront them should give them no undue cause for concern.

'We had fighter escort all the way to the target - Bf.109s and FW 190s ' was the cynical quip made by USAAF crews returning from their deep penetration daylight raids. Their aircraft waiting in the background, Messerschmitt Bf.109 pilots stand chatting until they get word of the raider's approach.

The Rumanian oil fields at Ploesti supplied Germany with fifty percent of its crude oil requirements. Beyond the range of Allied bombers based in Britain, the Ploesti oilfields were safe from air attack unless the B-24s of the USAAF 9th Air Force could contemplate a 2,000-mile round trip from their bases in North Africa.

According to the latest intelligence available, the fighter defences would not be strong, and most of the fighters would be flown by Rumanian pilots who were not terribly committed to the war. The anti-aircraft defences consisted of no more than 80 heavy ack-ack guns, and about twice that number of lighter calibre. At low level the heavy ack-ack should not trouble the attackers, and the light ack-ack was 'largely disposed for night attack.' It was not made clear how this would make them less of a threat to aircraft at low level in daylight. In any case, all the guns were manned by Rumanians – they said – who might well not stay at their posts in the face of a major attack. To help them make up their minds extra guns would be carried in the nose of the lead aircraft of each Allied formation.

At first light on Sunday, August 1, the first aircraft, carrying the mission navigator, rolled down the runway in Libya and headed for the first turning point, the island of Corfu, three hours flying time away in the Mediterranean. It was followed by one hundred and seventy seven others. Each carried extra fuel in an overload tank fitted in the bomb bay, along with a bomb load of around 4,000 lbs. Between them they had over 1,700 souls on board, and 311 tons of bombs. The bombs were fitted with delayed-action fuses so that the later aircraft in the formations would not be caught by the explosions of the bombs which had already been dropped. Heading the formation was 376th B.G., with twenty-nine aircraft. This was followed by 93rd, with thirty-nine aircraft, then by the forty-seven of 98th. Next came 44th's thirty-seven, and finally the 'rookie' Group, twenty-six Liberators of 389th.

Left: Liberators of 44th Bomb Group run in to their target at Ploesti - the Columbia Aquila refinery. The 44th were confused to find their target aleady in flames when they arrived. It had been attacked by 93rd Bomb Group, arriving over Ploesti from the wrong direction and unable to find their own target. Out of the sixteen Liberators of the 44th that flew into the smoke of the bombs dropped by the 93rd, only seven emerged.

As the elements of the raid were carried out in the wrong sequence, crews were faced with the unexpected hazard of their target (below left) being wreathed in smoke. Somewhere in the murk are factory chimneys and barrage balloons.

A Liberator is dramatically highlighted against the clouds of dense black smoke from which it has just emerged.

During their low-level training over Libya the B-24s and their engines had ingested the sands of the desert, and the resulting wear quickly began to tell as the formation set course for Corfu. Immediately after take off one of 98th's aircraft turned back with an engine on fire. The dust of the mass departure had still not settled, and the aircraft crashed making a blind landing, with the loss of all but two of the crew. Before the formation reached the first turning point ten aircraft had unloaded their bombs into the sea and turned for home with mechanical problems. Just short of Corfu, for no apparent reason, the lead aircraft, carrying the mission navigator, fell from the sky and plunged into the Mediterranean. This was going to have a dramatic effect on the whole outcome of the operation, especially as his wing man, carrying the deputy navigator, dropped down to look for survivors, then found that he could not catch up with the formation and turned for home.

Further problems beset 'Tidal Wave' as it reached Albania. The 9,000 ft peaks of the Pindis Mountains were shrouded in cumulus clouds. Penetrating the cloud in formation would involve the use of time-wasting standard safety procedures. Colonel K.K. Compton led 376th and 93rd in a climb to 16,000 ft, where they slipped through the cloud tops, maintaining formation visually. Colonel John Kane, leading 98th, decided that the climb would waste fuel, and decided to go through at 12,000 ft, giving him ample clearance over the peaks. Followed by 44th and 389th, he adopted the standard procedures to avoid collision while flying blind, and plunged into the cloud. This all took time, and, aided by a stronger tail wind 5,000 feet higher up, the leading two groups had disappeared from view by the time the others emerged and closed up again. Down below they spotted Bulgarian fighters, archaic aircraft which could not reach the height of the Liberators, but which would be sending early warning of the approaching attackers. With the gap that had split the formations, it was obviously no longer going to be possible to make either a surprise or a concerted attack on Ploesti. At this point it was pointless maintaining radio silence, but the formations did so, when perhaps they would have been better off reassembling the formations for the attack.

Sixty-five miles short of Ploesti, 389th turned

The 98th Bomb Group were briefed to run in to their target along the line of a railway, only to find that it was occupied by a flak train which took a heavy toll of the low-flying Liberators. When the surviving aircraft reached the target area, it had already been attacked, and they were faced with the additional hazard of exploding delayed-action bombs.

The burly shape of the Liberator's side view is belied by this overhead shot, revealing the elegant high-aspect ratio, low-drag wing, which contributed so much to its success.

away from the main formation to head for their own target, eighteen miles outside the Ploesti complex. Shortly afterwards the leading groups came to Targoviste, the last check point before Floresti, where the formation was due to make its final turn to make the run in to the target. The lead aircraft headed on for Floresti, but Colonel Compton, carrying Brigadier General U.G. Ent, the mission commander, mistook the town below for Floresti, and turned. The rest of of the aircraft followed. Many of the crews were aware of the error, but to fly straight on, when a massed formation of sixty or more aircraft around you were turning, was to invite collision. Radio silence was at last abandoned. Several pilots called out the mistake, but Compton carried on, leading the formation not towards Ploesti, but to Bucharest, a city protected by the strongest anti-aircraft defences in Europe.

Lieutenant Colonel Addison Baker, leading 93rd B.G. in the wake of the lead group, was also aware of the mistake. When he saw the spires and gunfire of Bucharest, he executed a ninety degree turn, to head directly for Ploesti. The rest of 93rd followed him, but they were now approaching their target from the south, instead of the west. The bombardiers found things totally different from the way they had looked when they had studied the target model from the correct direction. First they had to reach Ploesti. They had not completely avoided the Bucharest defensive ring – and it was not the puny Rumanian-manned affair that they had been told to expect. They entered an inferno of the dreaded 88 mm ack-ack guns, manned by German crews, and supported by a balloon barrage. Hit by a series of 88s Baker's 'plane became a blazing torch leading 93rd onto the target, where it crashed to become the pyre of the whole crew.

Meanwhile, the one aircraft that had followed the correct route had received the full attention of the guns, and of Messerschmitt fighters. The navigator was killed by a direct hit from an 88, which almost severed the pilot's leg. Three of the four engines were stopped – two of them on fire. They jettisoned their bombs, operated the fire extinguishers, and managed to land the crippled Liberator. Amazingly, all but two of the crew, including the pilot, survived, and became prisoners of the Rumanians and Germans.

The three groups that had been delayed over the mountains followed their briefing instructions, but became involved in the chaos which had developed over Ploesti. Some groups attacked targets which had been allocated to other groups; some actually bombed their own. Some bombed targets that had not been allocated at all, but in the circumstances anything that looked like an oil installation was fair game. Some formations found others looming out of the smoke, on a collision course, and had to bomb and take avoiding action at the same time.

Then the survivors had to make their way home. If things had gone according to plan the Liberators would have bombed in close formation, then swept on back towards Libya with the benefit of the mutual defence that the formation offered. Instead they headed back to make the Mediterranean crossing piecemeal. Some of them attempted to reform, but it was mainly small, vulnerable groups that fought their way back towards the long sea crossing.

In Benghazi they had received General Ent's 'Mission successful' signal, and waited the return of 'Tidal Wave' with excitement. The return of the scattered B-24s came as something of a shock. The mission had been successful: 'Tidal Wave' had reached Ploesti, and had hit the target. It was estimated that it had achieved sixty percent destruction, and 'put a serious dent in Germany's oil supply.' But it might also have been said, 'With a success like that, who needs a failure?' Fourteen of the aircraft which took off failed to make the target area. Of those that did, forty one were lost to enemy action, either over the target or on the way home. Less than forty of those which returned to Libya were still airworthy.

When the Allies had obtained a foothold in Italy they had bases from which they could attack Ploesti with fighter escort all the way. A year later the oilfield was finally knocked out, after a total of twenty-three attacks, and at a cost of 270 aircraft. Although 1,000 of the aircrew who were reported killed or missing during these raids were prisoners, who were repatriated when the Russians overran the Balkans, that still left more than 1,200 known killed or not accounted for.

Many of the Liberators made forced landings as they left the target area, or before they had escaped from Rumanian airspace. By the end of the day more than 150 American airmen either lay in Rumanian hospitals, or were in prison camps.

A dramatic shot of a B-24 emerging from the man-made overcast, as a sheet of flame erupts from the buildings below. The narrow margin of clearance between wing tip and chimney top can be seen quite clearly.

THE MARIANAS TURKEY SHOOT

In the air battle, a form of warfare unique to the 20th century, success or failure has always been dependent upon the finely balanced combination of the men and machines sent into battle by the antagonists. The balance has seldom been simply a matter of weight of numbers, but of a combination of the expertise of the men and the technical superiority of the machines. A single factor has often been sufficient to swing the balance, when in all other respects the two sides have been equal. In World War I such an event was the introduction of guns synchronised to fire through the arc of the propeller.

At the time of Pearl Harbor the Japanese had the ascendancy over America because their airmen had the advantage of experience in their war with the Chinese, whilst the American airmen were untried in combat. Also the American air forces were surprised by the capabilities of the Japanese aircraft. The American pilots, in their P.40s, and with no combat experience, were no match for the seasoned Japanese in their A6Ms, the redoubtable Zeros.

By 1944 the balance had swung the other way. The Japanese expansion through the Pacific and Indian Oceans had been extravagant in its wastage of aircraft and aircrews, while America had been learning from experience. The United States Navy Air Force now had a wealth of experienced aircrew, and aircraft which were well tried and at least a match for the latest version of the Zero. The majority of the Japanese aircrews were novice replacements.

From an all-time low after Pearl Harbor, the U.S. Navy's strength in the Pacific increased steadily. Two aircraft carriers, one an Independence Class, and one an Essex Class, both their decks crammed with aircraft, lead a Task Force unit of the Third Fleet.

In 1941 the Japanese had both experienced pilots and superior aircraft. However, by 1944 most of the Japanese veterans had been lost, and their aircraft outclassed. The novice Japanese fighter pilots fell in waves, so that any of the land-based bombers which tried to attack were unescorted and vulnerable.

America was anxious to begin B-29 raids on the Japanese homeland. As they progressively recaptured the Pacific islands, they decided to bypass Truk and the Carolines, and leap forward to the Marianas, from where they would be able to begin those operations. At the same time, the Japanese had devised a plan to lure the American Fleet into the area of the Carolines, where it would be trapped between their fleet and their shore-based aircraft. The scene was set for a showdown.

The overall command of the American plan was in the hands of Admiral Raymond Spruance, commanding the US Fifth Fleet. The Fifth Fleet was the largest and most powerful fleet in naval history, and depended heavily on the use of air power. Here the aircraft carrier had already become the capital ship of the 20th century. The fleet's striking force was Task Force 58, commanded by Rear Admiral Marc Mitscher.

Mitscher's force was divided into five elements. Task Groups 58.1 to 58.4 were carrier task groups with up to two fleet carriers and two light carriers each, and Task Group 58.7 was based around a group of seven fast battleships. The elements of TF. 58 could be used either as a unified Task Force, or as separate entities, allowing for groups to be detached to refuel and replenish without interrupting operations.

On June 11, 1944, TF 58 began to wear down the defences of the Marianas, in preparation for the landings. Their four Carrier Task Groups carried over 450 Hellcat fighters, and large formations of these were despatched over the islands to draw the Japanese aircraft into combat. By the end of the day they had destroyed 80 aircraft in combat and a further 30 on the ground. Their own losses had been only 21 Hellcats. By June 15 TF 58 had achieved sufficient air supremacy to launch the invasion, and 140,000 troops were landed by the Fifth Fleet on the islands of Saipan and Guam.

On the same day the Japanese main fleet sailed from the Suli Archipelago and joined up with the Mobile Fleet, under Vice Admiral Jisaburo Ozawa. Ozawa detached a force, under Vice-Admiral Kurita, with three light carriers, four battleships, five cruisers and eight destroyers. This fleet was the bait which, it was

Left: a Grumman Avenger torpedo bomber on the flight deck of the USS *Lexington*. The Avenger had entered service in 1942 and by June 1944 it had an established reputation with both the U.S. Navy and the Fleet Air Arm of the British Navy.

The anti-aircraft gunners (below left) of the Third Fleet had learned to give a good account of themselves by the last year of the war. Any bomber that broke through the screen of defensive fighters still had the Fleet's barrage to contend with.

The men on board the USS *Birmingham* (right) have not bothered to don their steel helmets, as they watch their fighter pilots have a field day 30,000 feet above, turning the sky into a reproduction of the skies over London four years earlier.

Below right: almost obscured by smoke and flame, a Japanese 'Betty' sinks off Saipan. This was one of fourteen Japanese planes brought down by anti-aircraft fire during the battle.

Left: a striking picture of a Helldiver (SB2C) peeling off to come in for a landing on its carrier's flight deck.

Below left: the Grumman Hellcat became the mainstay of the carrier-based fighters in the Pacific, beginning to replace the Wildcat during 1943. The *Essex* and the *Independence* were the first two carriers to embark the Hellcat.

Landing accidents on the carriers were often spectacular. A damaged and weakened Hellcat (below far right) has been ripped apart as its hook engaged the arrester wire. The pilot is being rescued from his cockpit, and the wreckage bulldozed over the side before the next aircraft can come home to roost.

One Helldiver (below right, top and bottom) has missed the arrester wires altogether, and has been brought to a halt by the wire barrier. The whirling propeller hurls splinters of wood from the flight deck and, as the engine is wrenched from its mountings, the broken fuel lines spray burning fuel back over the cockpits.

hoped, would lure the Americans within range of the main fleet, poised 100 miles behind it.

The two fleets jockeyed for position, and tried to keep track of the enemy force's movements. TF 58 made some use of reconnaissance aircraft, but relied mainly on reports from submarines and the direction finders at Pearl Harbor. These reports suggested that the Japanese were about 400 miles west-southwest of where TF 58 lay, off the Marianas. Mitscher wished to steam in that direction, to be better placed for an attack, but Spruance decided that his primary function was to protect the landings at Saipan and Guam, so they did not fall into the Japanese trap.

Early in the morning of June 19, Ozawa began flying off search aircraft, and by 8.30 a.m. he had enough information to launch his first strike. By 10 a.m. he had launched three strikes, totalling over 250 aircraft, of which about half were Zeros. The radar on board the American ships detected the approach of the strikes at 150 miles range, giving them plenty of time to get their fighters into the air. Most of the Hellcat pilots had been with the fleet for two years or more and were experienced veterans;

the majority of the Japanese were new to combat and proved to be no opposition for the TF 58 men. At debriefing one of them remarked, 'It's as easy as shooting turkeys.' The idea stuck. The battle became known as 'The Great Marianas Turkey Shoot'.

Those Japanese aircraft not shot down over the fleet went on to land at Guam or Tinian, in the Marianas, to refuel to return to their ships. TF 58's aircraft, patrolling over the islands, caught them as they were landing. Ozawa lost 218 aircraft, and finished the day with no more than 100 serviceable aircraft at his disposal. He had also had other problems while his strike aircraft had been away. The Japanese fleet had been attacked by submarines, which had sunk two of his carrier, including the *Taiho*, his flagship. He had been obliged to transfer his flag to the cruiser *Haguro*.

Returning to their carriers, the Japanese pilots made exaggerated claims of their successes, which left Ozawa with a picture more optimistic than the situation justified. He therefore hoped that he might still achieve a victory, and remained within reach of the

159

American fleet. He was found by Mitscher's searching aircraft the following afternoon. There would not be time to launch a strike and recover the aircraft before darkness fell over the carriers, but Mitscher was not prepared to risk losing his quarry. Over 200 aircraft were launched. A mixture of Hellcats, Helldivers and torpedo-carrying Avengers. Without the means to fight them off, Ozawa lost one of his remaining carriers and two of his refuellers. Two other carriers were severely damaged.

It was getting on for midnight before the strike returned to the fleet. Mitscher decided to take the risk of his fleet being within sight of any prowling Japanese craft, and ordered the whole fleet to light up. This enabled many of the aircraft to get down safely, but eighty or more of them either put down in the sea, or were destroyed in landing accidents. Thirteen aircrew were lost in landing or ditching.

At last Ozawa was convinced that he was beaten, and withdrew towards Okinawa.

The last great carrier battle of World War II was over.

Damage control and fire fighting were vital on a carrier, where thousands of gallons of aviation fuel were carried in tanks beneath the flight deck. Whether a fire was caused by enemy action or by a crashing plane, it had to be controlled at once.

KAMIKAZE-THE DIVINE WIND

The kamikaze pilots of the Japanese Navy, and their tokkatai counterparts of the Army Air Force, were treated with great ceremony. This was no undercover operation and numerous photographs such as this exist. The pilots parade to receive their final instructions.

In the 13th Century, a Mongol horde, led by Kublai Khan, was invading Japan supported by a vast fleet. Just as the defeat of the Japanese seemed certain, a typhoon sprang up. The Mongol fleet was scattered, and Japan was saved. The salvation was attributed to *Kamikaze*, the Divine Wind, sent by the Sun Goddess, Amaterasu Omikami. In 1944 Japan was outnumbered in both ships and aircraft; the American fleet and their allies were massing for the final series of assaults. Could Kamikaze blow once again, and stave off the inevitable?

It was becoming obvious that a major action in the Leyte Gulf, in the Philippines, was imminent. The part to be played by American carrier aircraft would be crucial, and Vice-Admiral Takijiro Ohnishi, Commander of the Japanese Naval Air Force's First Air Fleet, had the problem of neutralising the threat. The enemy's carrier task group had to be rendered ineffective for at least a week, to give the Japanese Second Fleet, a fleet without a single carrier of its own, a chance to get through to the Gulf to prey upon the American troop transports.

There was a high attrition rate among Japanese torpedo bombers and high-level bombers, and their success rate was minimal. Ohnishi had a plan to improve the return he was getting in exchange for his own losses. He paid a visit to the 201st Air Group, on the island of Luzon, to seek volunteers for a 'Special Attack Group'. The 201st, equipped with Zeros, had been practicing the technique of 'skip bombing' – approaching an enemy ship at high speed and low level – to launch a 250kg bomb which would bounce off the water and bury itself in the side of the ship, above its armour plating. The Special Attack Group would modify the technique slightly. They would not release their bomb, but would fly with it, to plunge both themselves and their bomb into the side of their target. This would greatly increase their accuracy. Most air forces could cite examples, in both World Wars, of airmen making the supreme sacrifice at a crucial moment in an air battle, but this had always been a spur of the moment action, in the heat of battle. Ohnishi's pilot sacrifice was to be premeditated and organised.

Some of the deficiencies of the first 'Zeros' were corrected in the ultimate version, the A6M5 (left), but it still did not achieve superiority over the Hellcats. It was, however, still a formidable weapon in the hands of a pilot who was committed to the death.

The Japanese planned to replace the 'Zero' with the A7M Reppu (Hurricane) (below left), code-named 'Sam' by the Allies. Fortunately it did not emerge from the production line in time to join the onslaught of the Divine Wind. With a planned diving speed of 550 mph, it would have been difficult to stop either by fighter interception or by anti-aircraft gunfire.

Right: another flattop, the USS *Kitkun Bay*, receives the attention of the kamikazes. This time the suicide plane has received a direct hit, and appears to be diving into the sea alongside its intended target.

There was no shortage of volunteers from the pilots of 201st Air Group. They went to work almost immediately. From 20 October their aircraft ranged the Philippines, seeking the elusive American carriers. Their first success came on October 25. Five Zeros carrying bombs, with four others flying escort, located a carrier group, and attacked. All five Kamikazes were successful in hitting carriers. The escort carrier *St. Lo* received hits from two of the Zeros and sank, earning the doubtful privilege of becoming the first victim of the new 'Divine Wind' which had begun to blow.

Other units were added to 201st, to form the 'Special Attack Corps', and from then on the American fleet was subjected to daily Kamikaze attacks. By the end of January 1945 the Kamikazes operating out of the Philippines had made over 400 sorties, and had lost 380 aircraft. In the process they had sunk 16 more ships, including another carrier, and had damaged almost 90 others, 17 of them capital

The crewmen on the bridge of an attacked ship stare anxiously into the smoke, hoping to spot the next kamikaze in time either to engage it or to take avoiding action.

Before a mission, the suicide squads went through a ceremony based on the rites of the ancient samurai. After receiving a final libation, the pilot was helped by a comrade to don the samurai headband symbolizing courage and composure.

ships – battleships, carriers or cruisers. Ohnishi became so convinced of the comparative effectiveness of the 'special attack' technique that he extended it to all the aircraft of the First Air Fleet; bombers and torpedo bombers, as well as the 'Zeros. He also preached the doctrine to the commander of the Second Air Fleet, Vice-Admiral Shigeru Fukudome. Eventually Fukudome reluctantly agreed, and the Second Air Fleet was added to the Special Attack Corps.

Vice-Admiral Ohnishi was not the only one who had had the idea of suicide missions. During the summer of 1944 a junior officer, Ensign Ohta, an air transport pilot flying out of Rabaul, had drawn up plans for a piloted rocket-propelled bomb. His idea was considered by Navy High Command and the Aeronautics Department. Experiments were carried out with all speed, and by the end of 1944 the Yokosuka MXY 7, the Okha (Cherry Blossom) had been put into production. Built

principally of wood, the Ohka carried a warhead of 1,800kg of explosive, and was powered by five rocket motors, which would hurl it towards its target at over 600 mph. It was to be carried, beneath a Mitsubishi G4M 'Betty' land bomber to within twenty miles of its target, when the pilot would operate the release and fire the engines for the final approach. The Americans called the Ohka the 'Baka' (foolish) bomb. It first appeared during operations in the Okinawa area, during the summer of 1945. Fortunately for the fleet, the Betty, with its flying bomb on board, was very slow and unmanoeuverable, and vulnerable to the American carrier fighters. The Japanese did not have the resources in fighter aircraft to provide the Bettys with sufficient escorts to make certain that they could deliver their Baka safely to the release point.

The techniques of the 'special attack' were studied, and a training programme was instituted for the volunteer pilots. The flight was divided into three phases, and training was given to prepare the pilot for the particular demands of each phase. The main problem during the takeoff phase was the need for it to be carried out as quickly as possible. Since the plan to prevent the Allied landings at Leyte had failed, the Kamikaze bases were now within range of American land based bombers. The Special Attack aircraft were dispersed around the airfields, and camouflaged, to minimise the risk of them being destroyed on the ground. The first two days of the training programme were devoted to the practice of getting quickly and safely from the hide and into the air. This was followed by two days of intensive training in formation flying. It was obvious that if the Kamikazes and their escorts arrived over the target area en masse, the defenders would have much greater difficulty in dealing with them than if they arrived piecemeal. Finally, the trainees spent three days studying the problems of the approach to the target, angle of attack, and target selection.

In the spring and early summer of 1945, by which time operations had moved to the Okinawa area, both Navy and Army Air Forces were carrying out suicide missions. It was decided that their efforts should be coordinated. This resulted in a series of mass attacks, designated 'Kikusui' (floating chrysanthemum) operations. The first and biggest of these, on April 6/7, put 355 Kamikazes

Right: there can be no doubt as to the intention of the pilot of this Aichi D3A 'Val' dive bomber as it hurtles towards a U.S. cruiser. Unless a lucky last-second direct hit explodes the 'Val' in mid air, there is now no way that the ship can avoid serious damage.

Overleaf: a kamikaze 'Zero' about to plunge into the side of a U.S. capital ship. The photograph is believed to have been taken from the bridge of the battleship USS *Missouri*, which was damaged by kamikaze attacks in the Okinawa area on April 11 and 16, 1945.

into the air. Although more than 200 were shot down before reaching the fleet, those that got through inflicted considerable damage. Four ships were sunk, and twenty-five more, including a battleship and a carrier, were damaged.

There was, by now, a change in the attitude of the pilots. In the early days the Special Attack Corps had been made up entirely of volunteers, filled with a spirit of spontaneous enthusiasm. Now the enthusiasm was beginning to wane, and pressure was having to be brought to encourage 'volunteers'. This meant that the flying training period had to be preceded by a period of indoctrination.

All was to no avail. The Divine Wind had not prevented the landings at Leyte, and it did not prevent the defeat of the defenders of Okinawa. Now the American forces had moved to within reach of the Japanese homeland. Japan braced itself for invasion, but it was not to come. American B-29s could now fly missions over Japan with much less risk than their soldiers and marines would face storming the beaches. The Allies believed that the end was in sight, and at the end of July an ultimatum was published, demanding immediate unconditional surrender of the armed forces of Japan. The demand was rejected. Leaflets were dropped on eleven Japanese cities, telling them that they were in danger of intensive aerial bombardment, and on July 28 six of them were bombed. Twelve more cities were

The Yokosuka MXY7 Ohka, a piloted flying bomb, the ultimate weapon of the kamikaze pilot, code-named 'Baka' by the Allies. The Ohka had a range of little more than twenty miles, and was carried to within range of its target by a 'mother aircraft', usually a Mitsubishi G4M 'Betty'.

170

Besides the damage inflicted by the war load of the suicide aircraft, its fuel tanks acted as an enormous incendiary device. This gasoline-fired inferno was photographed during an attack on the USS Intrepid.

warned on July 31, and, as the ultimatum was still not accepted, four of them were bombed on August 1. The final warning was given on August 5. The U.S. Army Air Force had dropped a million and a half leaflets each day, and three million copies of the ultimatum. Then came America's own Divine Wind; on August 6 at Hiroshima, and again on the 9th at Nagasaki.

On August 15 a public announcement was made of Japan's acceptance of the ultimatum. That evening, in the study on the second floor of his residence, Vice-Admiral Takijiro Ohnishi joined the men of his Special Attack Corps,

performing *hara-kiri* – ritual suicide – with his ceremonial sword. His Divine Wind had not prevented his nation's defeat, and the Allies victory in Japan was added to their victory in Europe, three months earlier.

World War II was over. It had begun with a German air raid on Poland; it ended with an American air raid on Japan. The prophesy made by Britain's Winston Churchill had come true. There had been many disasters, there had been immeasurable cost and tribulation, but in the end there had been Victory.

By the time the kamikaze battle was launched, it was already too late for it to alter the outcome of the war, which came to a violent end with the entry of the 'Enola Gay'. This B-29 bomber carried 'Little Boy', the atomic bomb which was dropped on Hiroshima on August 6, 1945.

The mushroom cloud which resulted from the explosion of 'Fat Boy', the second atomic weapon, dropped on Nagasaki three days after the explosion in Hiroshima.

The total devastation (overleaf) created by the atomic explosions convinced the Japanese civil power to overule the military authorities and accept the unconditional surrender demanded by the Allies to bring World War II to an end.

BIBLIOGRAPHY

The Encyclopedia of Air Warfare (Salamander 1975)

ANGELUCCI AND MATRICIADI, World Aircraft (Sampson, Low and Mondaradi 1977)

BROWN, SHORES AND MACKSEY, The Guiness History of Air Warfare (Purnell 1976)

DENIS RICHARDS, The Royal Air Force 1939-1945 Vol. 1 The Fight at Odds (HMSO 1953)

DENIS RICHARDS AND H. ST. G. SAUNDERS, The Royal Air Force 1939-1945 Vol.2 The Fight Avails (HMSO 1953)

H. ST. G. SAUNDERS, The Royal Air Force 1939-1945 Vol. 3 The Fight is Won (HMSO 1954)

AIR MINISTRY PAMPHLET NO. 248, The Rise and Fall of the German Air Force (Air Ministry 1948)

JOHN MASEFIELD, The Nine Days Wonder (The Operation Dynamo) (Heinemann 1941)

A.J. BARKER, Dunkirk, The Great Escape (Dent 1977)

FRANCIS K. MASON, Battle over Britain (McWhirter 1989)

ARTHUR WARD, A Nation Alone (Osprey 1989)

ALAN C. DEERE, Nine Lives (Hodder and Stoughton 1959)

WINSTON S. CHURCHILL, The Second World War (Cassell)
     Vol. I The Gathering Storm (1948)
     Vol. II Their Finest Hour (1949)
     Vol. III The Grand Alliance (1950)
     Vol. IV The Hinge of Fate (1951)
     Vol. V Closing the Ring (1952)
     Vol. VI Triumph and Tragedy (1954)

MINISTRY OF INFORMATION FOR THE AIR MINISTRY, The Air Battle of Malta (HMSO 1944)

MINISTRY OF INFORMATION FOR THE ADMIRALTY, Fleet Air Arm (HMSO 1943)

EDWARD JABLONSKI, Tragic Victories (Doubleday 1971)

QUENTIN REYNOLDS, The Amazing Mr. Doolittle (Cassell 1954)

CARROLL V. GLINES, Doolittle's Tokyo Raiders (Van Nostrand 1964)

AIR STAFF HEADQUARTERS A.C.S.E.A., Air Transport Operations on the Burma Front (Air Command South East Asia 1944)

PUBLIC RELATIONS SECTIONS, E.A.C., Burma Air Victory (Eastern Air Command 1945)

PETER M. BOWERS, Boeing B-17 Flying Fortress (Museum of Flight 1985)

GUY GIBSON V.C., Enemy Coast Ahead (Michael Joseph 1955)

PAUL BRICKHILL, The Dam Busters (Evans Bros. 1951)

JOHN SWEETMAN, Schweinfurt: Disaster in the Skies (Ballantine Books 1971)

THOMAS M. COFFEY, Decision over Schweinfurt (David McKay 1977)

DUGAN AND STEWART, Ploesti (Random House 1962)

INOGUCHI, NAKAJIMA AND PINEAU, The Divine Wind (Hutchinson 1959)